Goldendo

Edie MacKenzie

B.E.S.
PUBLISHING

Contents

Introduction

The Goldendoodle is a purposefully bred hybrid that, unfortunately, is lumped into the category of "designer dog." However, the Goldendoodle is not a designer dog, but rather, a dog of good design.

A Goldendoodle results from the deliberate breeding of a Golden Retriever and a Poodle. Goldendoodles are smart. Just how smart are they? Consider this: The American Kennel Club lists the Poodle as the second smartest dog. The Golden Retriever is no slouch either, coming in at number four. The key to owning any highly intelligent dog is knowing that they require more training and more mental stimulation than other dogs because their agile minds, when not given proper direction, use canine logic to creatively figure things out. This can lead to less desirable behaviors. But focused, persistent training during your Goldendoodle's first year will yield years of enjoyment.

In addition to intelligence, the AKC lists the energy level of both the Golden Retriever and the Poodle as "Very Active." As a result, Goldendoodles need not only intellectual stimulation and proper training, but a lot of exercise as well. Their energy and athleticism have led them to excel in a wide variety of competitive canine sports.

Goldendoodles have intuitive, sensitive natures—a genetic gift from their Golden Retriever parent. If you decide to bring a Goldendoodle into your life, be prepared to spend a lot of time with her. They are very people oriented and need a lot of human interaction. Luckily, the Goldendoodle's Poodle parent often contributes a non-shedding, allergy-friendly coat, making the Goldendoodle an ideal pet for many homes. Due to their intelligence, playfulness, and potentially allergy-friendly coats, Goldendoodles are one of the most popular hybrid breeds.

The Goldendoodle was developed to serve as an allergy-friendly service and therapy dog. The breed has successfully provided assistance to people in need who suffer from dander-related dog allergies.

Like so many other dogs, most Goldendoodles live their lives as beloved pets rather than as working dogs. However, this does not negate the importance and life-changing benefits this breed brings to those who need an allergy-friendly dog with a willingness to serve.

The intelligence and intuitive nature of the Goldendoodle comes into play during training. They are quick learners and shine in any kind of training environment.

Goldendoodles also love to please. They have a way of tilting their head and looking at you, as if trying to figure out what you want next. Your Goldendoodle will learn to read you like a book. It is up to you to send her the right messages.

While the Goldendoodle's high intelligence can lead to boredom and, therefore, mischief, well-bred Goldendoodles have easygoing personalities, which makes them wonderful dogs for young families or first-time dog owners. That said, it is imperative for someone without dog experience to get expert advice from his or her breeder, an accredited dog trainer, and a caring veterinarian.

The goal of this book is to give the new-to-dog's owner, or soon-to-be owner, an educational foundation to build upon. So, let's begin by exploring whether a Goldendoodle is the right dog for you and your family.

Characteristics of the Goldendoodle

The Goldendoodle is NOT a hypoallergenic dog—no dog breed is. People can be allergic to dog saliva or dog dander, which is spread when a dog's fur sheds. The Goldendoodle, when its coat is nonshedding, is an allergy-friendly dog.

The Goldendoodle is a hybrid dog created by mating a Golden Retriever with a Poodle—either a Standard Poodle or one of the three smaller poodle variations, the Moyen/Klein, Miniature, or Toy. Modern breeding relies on genetic testing and careful breeding to create dogs of optimal health. Golden Retrievers and Poodles have a variety of potential genetic defects in common, and the Golden Retriever has a strong genetic tendency toward cancer. It is only through careful breeding that these defects can be weeded out to ensure a healthy Goldendoodle.

THE GOLDENDOODLE TEMPERAMENT

A well-bred Goldendoodle is happy and affectionate with a zestful "life of the party" personality. Goldendoodles are also eager to please and will make a great deal of eye contact trying to figure out what you want them to do. Combine all of this with their high level of intelligence, and you get a breed that is relatively easy to train. However, their intelligence and enthusiastic nature require diligence on your part. Contrary to popular belief, a highly intelligent dog requires more training and more stimulation than a dog of average intelligence. When properly trained, Goldendoodles are very adaptable to a family environment and can make good companions for children. But keep in mind, their strong retriever parentage makes them mouthy. Their mouths are most active when they are puppies, and your Goldendoodle will use her mouth on you or your children if not properly trained. An easy way to train your Goldendoodle is to work with her natural tendency to retrieve items. Whenever she gets mouthy with you or a family member, put a favorite toy in her mouth; in no time she'll be grabbing a toy each time she approaches you or starts to feel frisky.

All puppies, no matter the breed, are busy and active. Goldendoodles are no exception. Often, their mellow, calm temperament becomes more apparent as they approach maturity. This is why it is essential to work with a breeder who is actively breeding for good health and calm temperaments.

It is critical for prospective owners to take their time to research and interview breeders before purchasing a puppy. All puppies are cute. Sadly, not all puppies are healthy, nor are all breeders honest and ethical. The work you put in to locate a reputable, responsible Goldendoodle breeder goes a long way toward bringing a happy, healthy Goldendoodle into your family. Ideally, breeders of Goldendoodles breed for sound, genetically healthy dogs with good, gentle temperaments and low- to nonshedding coats. You must do your due diligence, as the popularity of the Goldendoodle motivates many unscrupulous breeders. Carefully read the section later in this chapter on how to choose a breeder on page 10. It will make a significant difference in the quality of the dog you take home.

GOLDENDOODLE COAT TYPES

As a general rule, the curlier the coat, the less likely it is to shed and spread allergens. The Goldendoodle's hair grows to four to six inches long and usually has a wavy or curly look to it. In the early days of Goldendoodles, coat type could be a hit or a miss. Today, using genetic testing, your breeder can give you an accurate description of your puppy's adult coat based on length, curl, and probability of shedding.

TYPES OF GOLDENDOODLES

The term "Goldendoodle" covers a multitude of Golden Retriever/Poodle/Goldendoodle combinations. Goldendoodles are identified by two distinct categories. The first, and most apparent, variable is size. The other variable is generations. But to make matters just a bit more complicated, each size can also have generational variables.

What Size?

Not sure which size matches the dog you want, but have a clear picture in your mind? Simply take a tape measure and measure your leg from the floor to where you imagine the shoulders of your full-grown Goldendoodle.

Size

A dog's size is measured at the withers, not at the top of the head. The withers are the highest part of the back at the base of the neck.

According to the Goldendoodle Association of North America (GANA), Goldendoodles fall into four size categories:

- Standard Range: Height at the withers over 21 inches (53 cm); weight 51 pounds (23 kg) or more.
- Medium Range: Height at the withers over 17 inches (43 cm) but under 21 inches (53 cm); weight 36–50 pounds (16–23 kg).
- Miniature Range: Height at the withers over 14 inches (36 cm) but under 17 inches (43 cm); weight 26–35 pounds (12–16 kg).
- Petite Range: Height at the withers below 14 inches (36 cm); weight generally 25 pounds (11 kg) or less.

Reprinted with permission from Goldendoodle Association of North America (GANA), 2018.

Generations

Until recent advances in canine genetic testing allowed for significantly higher levels of accuracy in terms of coat length, curl, furnishings, and nonshedding in the first breeding of a Golden Retriever and a Poodle, many breeders relied on the antiquated concept of hybrid vigor and their own experience with their breeding dogs. Hybrid vigor derives from the idea that the offspring of two unrelated breeds of the same species will receive all of the parents' good traits and few of the bad. This works as long as the parent breeds do not have a common gene for a genetic defect.

Genetic testing for coat type has eliminated the need for additional backcrossing and multiple generations in breeding. However, there are many good breeders, prior to the availability of genetic testing for coat type, who invested a tremendous amount of time and energy to develop health-tested breeding lines that produce consistently reliable nonshedding coats—and the quality of the dogs they breed should not be discounted. So, let's take a look at the various generations of Goldendoodles. You can work with either a breeder who does genetic testing for coat quality and/or a long-time breeder whose experience and commitment has also resulted in top-quality Goldendoodles.

It is critical that both breeding parents and, ideally, the previous generations are tested for, and pass, all the potential genetic defects and diseases (see "Health and Wellness," pages 44–46).

F1 The breeding of a Golden Retriever with one of the following four sizes of Poodle—Standard, Moyen/Klein (medium), Miniature, and Toy—results in a litter of F1 puppies or First Generation. "F" stands for the Latin word *filial* or *generation*. Both Golden Retrievers and Poodles have the recessive gene for long coats; therefore, F1 Goldendoodles carry two genes for long coats. Because of the two long coat genes, many Goldendoodle breeders don't breed beyond the initial pairing of the Golden Retriever and the Poodle.

F1b The F1b Goldendoodle is the breeding of an F1 Goldendoodle backcrossed (b) with a Poodle. This yields a dog twenty-five percent Golden Retriever and seventy-five percent Poodle. By adding more Poodle into the genetic mix, the likelihood of a curly, nonallergy-inducing coat is higher. As noted above, genetic testing for coat length, curl, furnishings, and nonshedding attributes now make this backcrossing unnecessary. However, not all breeders are up to speed with genetic testing for coat-related genes and may successfully produce reliable coats without genetic testing.

F2 The F2 Goldendoodle results when both parents are F1 Goldendoodles. While this yields a dog that is still fifty percent Golden Retriever and fifty percent Poodle, the F2 is a more genetically diverse dog than the F1. The primary advantage of F2 breeding is the ability to select the most desirable traits from a breeder's F1 Goldendoodles and reproduce them consistently.

Multigen According to GANA, the multigen (multiple generational) Goldendoodle is the result of breeding two Goldendoodles. However, unlike the F2, one of the multigen parents must be either an F1b Goldendoodle or another multigen Goldendoodle.

Additionally, a multigen Goldendoodle bred to a Poodle is also considered a multigen Goldendoodle.
Reprinted with permission from Goldendoodle Association of North America (GANA), 2018.

GOLDENDOODLE COLORS

Contrary to their name, Goldendoodles come in a variety of colors. With the advent of genetic testing for coat type, breeders are now also able to breed more consistently for color. The most common colors are cream and gold, but many Goldendoodles are also chocolate or black. Less common, but rather striking, are the red Goldendoodles. Parti Goldendoodles are generally white with large blocks of either black or brown. Goldendoodles occasionally have either black or chocolate phantom coloring. There is also the rare and beautiful silver color.

CHOOSING A BREEDER

It is important to purchase your puppy from a trustworthy and experienced breeder who thoroughly health tests all of his/her breeding dogs. This comes with a heftier cost. However, if you are looking for a top-quality Goldendoodle, price should be at the bottom of your priority list. You know you have found a good breeder if his/her mission is to produce healthy, sound, and well-tempered dogs. The research needed to find a good breeder can be a long, tedious process, but it's worth every minute when you find the right breeder who can provide you with the right Goldendoodle. Finding the right breeder is especially critical with Goldendoodles. There are countless backyard breeders who breed solely for the money, giving no real attention to the critical issues of health and temperament.

A reputable breeder strives to advance the quality of the puppies with each new litter. This breeder matches parent dogs (who pass all health tests) for desirable physical and behavioral characteristics to produce a healthy litter.

Visiting the breeder gives you an opportunity to meet the puppy's siblings and parents so you get an idea of the physical and behavioral characteristics. Pay close attention to the parents to see if they are healthy and well behaved. Also, ask about their temperament and if they've had any types of health issues. Take notice of how the puppies interact with the breeder. It is a good sign if they are playful and outgoing.

Should a Breeder Be a Member of a Regulatory Body?

If a breeder is a member of a regulatory organization, it means he/she agreed to a code of ethics. However, few organizations can actually follow through to investigate whether the breeder is adhering to the code of ethics, and are limited to feedback and complaints. The quality of the regulatory body is important. Too many breeder listings simply require the breeder to pay specified advertising fees.

There are many small, ethical, and responsible breeders who are not members of any regulatory organizations. However, this leaves you without proof that the necessary genetic testing has not only been done, but that the parents passed all the testing as well.

An example of a quality regulatory organization is the Goldendoodle Association of North America (GANA), *www. GoldendoodleAssociation.com*. GANA gives different levels of "ribbons" for member breeders who health test all their breeding dogs for specific diseases and genetic defects, with a blue ribbon indicating the breeder completed all recommended health testing. Breeders are required to register all administered tests and test results with GANA. If a GANA member has a parent dog that carries a genetic defect, GANA requires proof the dog chosen as the mate is tested and clear of the defective gene so no genetic linkup of the gene is passed onto the puppies. Additionally, all members are required to offer a minimum 2 year warranty for life-inhibiting genetic defects, and pledge to honor the GANA Breeder Code of Ethics.

If a breeder isn't with an organization, he/she should still be testing for all Golden Retriever genetic diseases and defects (and that list is quite long) and all Poodle genetic diseases and defects. Just be cautious if test results are not registered with a neutral third party. Be aware there are unscrupulous

breeders who use photo editing technology to change health scores and to create false "certificates" of health results. If you cannot look at the test results online, from either an independent testing organization such as OFA or a regulatory body such as GANA, walk away.

Health Guarantees and Testing

A health guarantee can be used to evaluate a breeder. Having all health tests done (see "Health and Wellness," pages 44–46) can mitigate the need for a health guarantee—to a point. Mistakes happen. A health guarantee gives the puppy buyer some recourse if his/her puppy's health is less than optimal. Read the breeder's health guarantee and contract

A Word About Puppy Mills

Unfortunately, puppy mills (large, commercial dog breeding facilities) are big business. Dogs are poorly treated, live in filthy, confined conditions, and receive little or no veterinary care. They don't get exercise, playtime, or companionship. They often endure mistreatment and malnutrition. When these dogs reproduce with each other, it results in a litter with severe genetic defects; the puppies are seldom healthy.

Puppy mills typically sell their dogs in one of three ways: on websites, in pet stores, or through brokers—who in turn sell the puppies to pet stores. While not all puppies sold in pet stores come from puppy mills, a disturbing number of them do; so before you purchase a Goldendoodle puppy from a pet store, ask for the name and address of the breeder or the breeding facility (not the broker who may be the go-between), and then go home and do some research. A quick Internet search will let you know if there are any complaints against the store.

Warning: Don't believe everything you see on breeder websites. Puppy mills are very savvy and know exactly how to present themselves online. They often steal photos from other websites or from social media accounts of Goldendoodle owners. They create a fictitious "home" in which the puppies supposedly live, claim the puppies are being raised with children, and say all the right things to lure you in.

For more information about puppy mills and how to avoid purchasing a puppy mill puppy (and thereby supporting this awful business), go to the Humane Society of the United States' site *www.stoppuppy-mills.org* or the America Society for the Prevention of Cruelty to Animals' (ASPCA) site *www.aspca.org* and search "puppy mills." Both sites give excellent information about how puppy mills operate and their sophisticated efforts to defraud consumers.

Warning! All puppies are cute, even cleaned up sick puppies from a puppy mill.

before you send a deposit. Many breeders and websites claim they guarantee their puppies but fail to follow through with any guarantee or provide you with a written/printable copy, which leaves you not knowing what is or isn't covered. Reputable breeders who are confident in their puppies are more than happy to provide this information before you send them any money. Read the health guarantee and contract *very* carefully, and make sure you are comfortable with all of the terms. For example, if a legitimate genetic defect is found, are you required to return your puppy to the breeder? Will the breeder refund a portion of your purchase price to help defray veterinary costs? What are you required to do while raising your puppy to stay in compliance with the terms of the health guarantee?

Also, does the health guarantee dictate when the puppy is desexed? When to spay or neuter your Goldendoodle is something you want to give some serious thought. Spaying and neutering is discussed in more detail in "Health and Wellness," page 49.

Understanding the breeder's health guarantee is critical. There are breeders whose health guarantees are for *fatal* genetic flaws only. Given that, it can be assumed hip dysplasia, elbow dysplasia, luxating patella, and a variety of eye issues, none of which are *fatal* genetic flaws, are not covered in the guarantee. This is not acceptable. As the owner of the puppy, ensure your interests are covered, not just the interests of the breeder.

There are also unscrupulous breeders who charge extra for a health guarantee or for regular veterinary checks. Again, this is not something reputable breeders do, and you, the consumer, need to exercise caution.

Questions to Ask the Breeder

Make sure to be well prepared with a list of questions when visiting or talking to Goldendoodle breeders. Here is a list of questions the breeder should be happy to answer for you. If he/she is not cooperative or acts annoyed, this is not the breeder for you. A good breeder wants you to ask questions and delights in sharing his/her knowledge and enthusiasm for Goldendoodles.

Why are you selling the puppies?
The breeder's response will give you a good idea if he/she is breeding for the love of Goldendoodles or just trying to get rich off a high-demand dog.

Are Tested Puppies Always Perfect?

Will a puppy coming from fully tested, registered parents cost more than a puppy coming from untested parents? Probably, and reasonably so. Testing is expensive. Comprehensive genetic health testing can cost thousands of dollars per breeding dog. Add to that the cost for genetic testing for coat, color, and furnishings, and the breeder has a significant investment in his/her breeding dogs. It comes down to the critical difference between price and cost. The monetary *price* of a puppy from untested parents may be cheaper; however, the long-term *cost*, both financial and emotional, of living with a chronically ill, disabled, or ill-tempered Goldendoodle is far higher than the price difference between the puppies of tested and untested parents. Think long and hard before you decide on your breeder and puppy.

How many breeding dogs do you own? How many litters per year do the females have and at what ages do they begin and end breeding?

Note: Breeding dogs should not be bred before two years of age because their hips cannot be accurately scored until that time. Females should not be bred past the age of seven.

What health testing is done on your breeding dogs? Are the results of the tests registered and posted online so I can access them?

How are the puppies socialized? Specifically, are they exposed to people, both adults and children, and other animals? How often are the puppies in social situations?

Are you working on early mental stimulation using problem solving toys, activities, or a puppy-sized playground?

What are prominent characteristics of the Goldendoodle temperament? What are the exercise requirements? Is it difficult to care for the Goldendoodle coat?

Ask many specific questions about the Goldendoodle breed, even if you already know the answers. This exercise will indicate how well he/she knows the breed.

Do you have any references?

If the breeder does not encourage or allow you to talk to previous customers, be concerned. Be sure to get several references and call or e-mail all of them.

What do you do if the puppy doesn't work in the new home? How involved are you in helping owners solve problems? Do you take dogs back with no questions asked? Do you refer to a rescue and rehome organization? Are you involved in GD rescue?

A breeder should be willing to work with a family to rehome a puppy that does not work out for them, particularly if the issue is related to allergies. If the issue is behavioral, the breeder should work with the family to find solutions. A breeder who is being asked to take a puppy back has every right to ask questions. He/she needs to understand the circumstances and how they may impact the next owner. If you are surrendering a puppy back to a breeder for something other than what is covered by your contract, do not have any expectation of a refund.

Breeder Research

There are many ways to check out breeders to ensure he/she is honest and producing quality litters.

You can:

- post an inquiry on one of the Goldendoodle forums listed in the Information section;
- search for Goldendoodle groups on social media, and ask for feedback on your list of potential breeders; check with the Better Business Bureau in the breeder's location; and/or
- ask one of the Goldendoodle rescue organizations—they know who to avoid and who is a good breeder.

What to Expect from a Breeder

Just as you expect to buy a high-quality puppy from a top-notch breeder, the breeder should expect to sell only to a reliable caretaker who will bring the puppy into a loving home. You should feel like you are being interviewed by the breeder for the privilege of taking this puppy home. The breeder should ask very specific questions to learn how you plan to care for the puppy. These questions

are your indication the breeder is sincerely concerned about the puppy's well-being. If the breeder seems more concerned about how you are going to pay for the puppy, then it is likely he/she is in the business for the wrong reasons.

When visiting, the breeder should require you to remove your shoes and thoroughly wash your hands before seeing and handling the puppies. The breeder should insist the puppy not leave her mother before eight weeks. It is important for the puppy to be close to her mother and littermates from ages four to eight weeks. She is learning how to interact, and if she's deprived of this essential developmental period, she could develop behavioral problems. Socialization with other people and animals should take place between six and twelve weeks of age.

When touring the breeder's home, pay attention. The environment should be clean and safe. Ask to see where the puppies sleep and play. Puppies should not be allowed outdoors until they are fully vaccinated.

The puppies should be clean and well fed but not fat, healthy, energetic, and social. If the puppies are dirty and foul smelling or have glassy eyes or runny noses, you should be apprehensive. And don't forget to check the cleanliness of the ears and the rectal area.

What to Expect on a Puppy Application

Expect to fill out a puppy application before purchasing your Goldendoodle. This form collects information about you and your family's desire for the puppy. Some potential questions are: *Why do you want a Goldendoodle? Have you ever owned or trained a dog before? Where will your puppy sleep? How many hours will she be left alone each day? What will you feed her?*

There will also be questions about your family dynamics, as well as questions about allergies within your family. At this point, you are usually required to pay a deposit when you submit an application or have an application interview. Typically, you pay the remainder of the fee when you take possession of the puppy. Again, make certain you have thoroughly read, and are comfortable with, the terms of the breeder's contract and health guarantee *before* you send any money.

RESCUED AND REHOMED GOLDENDOODLES

Are you interested in a rescued or a rehomed Goldendoodle? There are a lot of benefits and a few issues when bringing a rescue into your home, but the long-term love and affection is worth surmounting the

Parvo

When there is a parvo or a distemper outbreak in a region, a breeder may not allow you to visit the puppies. Be wary, though. Saying there is an outbreak in their region is a frequently used trick of puppy mills to keep people from visiting their facility. If you get this response, simply do an in-depth Internet search based on the breeder's location and the type of outbreak he/she claims is occurring. You can also call a local animal shelter or a local veterinarian. If there is no current record of an outbreak, steer clear of the breeder. That said, parvo is a deadly disease and extreme caution is understandable. If there is an outbreak in the region and the breeder is adamant about no visitors, do some additional research of the breeder's credentials and the regulatory bodies to which the breeder belongs. Ask for references from people who have been to the breeding facility. Also, in this age of technology, ask the breeder if he/she will provide a live virtual tour of his/her home and breeding facilities via your smartphone once a puppy application has been submitted. Hold the application fee until the virtual tour takes place.

challenges. You will find several foster-based Doodle rescue organizations, and some Golden Retriever rescue organizations, who also rescue Goldendoodles, listed in the Information section on page 91.

Working with a rescue organization that utilizes foster homes for their rescue dogs brings some wonderful benefits for the adopting family, particularly if this is a first ever dog. A foster family gets to know the dog, both the good and the not so good, and provides a clear picture of what type of family is best for that particular dog: kids/no kids, cats/no cats, other dogs/must be a solo dog, and so on. A foster family also works to train the rescue Doodle or shore up what training she may already have.

Reporting Abuse

If you see evidence of neglect and/or abuse of either the puppies or the parents, do not hesitate to contact the ASPCA at *www.aspca.org*. Your voice may be the only one for the neglected animals.

Loving foster homes make safe transitional places for dogs needing new homes without the trauma of being in a shelter. Foster homes also help shelter dogs, as well as dogs from hoarders and puppy mills, learn how to function in a home with a variety of social situations—often including children and other dogs—before moving on to their forever homes.

A rescue dog can come into foster care or a shelter tainted by the opinions of a previous owner. "Unfriendly, unlovable, and grouchy" is an actual quote from a relinquishing owner of a dog that, when placed in foster care, turned out to be a lovable, goofy, snuggly dog just waiting for the right family to find him. He's a very happy camper these days, living with his "foster failure" family—he was so sweet they adopted him!

Maybe it's anthropomorphizing, but rescue dog owners will tell you the bond they share with their dogs is a unique treasure: the dogs are grateful for caring owners who took a chance on them.

New Puppy, Now What?

You have decided to bring a Goldendoodle into your home. Are you ready? There are a lot of preparations you will need to make before you bring home your new bundle of fur.

BRINGING A PUPPY INTO THE FAMILY

When is the best time to bring a Goldendoodle into your family? This is a very personal decision. Ask yourself if there is enough time in your day to accommodate a puppy—not just now, but in five, ten, and fifteen years when she is a full-grown dog. For some families, the decision to add a puppy is an easy "yes." For others, sports, work schedules, school schedules, and any other number of activities outside the home make the answer a "no" to a puppy, but a "yes" to an older rescue or rehome. Be honest with yourself. A dog is a lifetime commitment.

BEFORE BRINGING YOUR PUPPY HOME

Plastic Crate vs. Wire Crate

Crates come in many different sizes and two varieties: hard plastic crates with "windows" for airflow, and wire crates, which are more open. Both crates are safe, functional choices for your puppy's home. Whichever crate style you choose, it must have two latches, top and bottom, on the door. A single latch in the center can be dangerous and potentially fatal if a dog forces her head into the upper or lower area; she can get stuck and cut off her air supply. If you plan to travel with your Goldendoodle, be aware airlines require the hard, plastic style.

Crate Comfort—Sweet Dreams

It is far too easy for an unattended Goldendoodle to not only chew up the bedding inside her crate, but also ingest it. This can have tragic consequences (see "Intestinal Blockages" on pages 59–60). A standard Goldendoodle is going to have a stronger ability to chew her bedding than a smaller Goldendoodle; however, you need to exercise caution when choosing the type of bedding you put in the crate with a puppy or a dog, regardless of her size. Until you are confident your Goldendoodle won't chew her bedding, put nothing but a thick layer of newspaper and a sturdy, chew-proof toy in the crate with her. Gradually move her to a bed without stuffing, and then to a regular bed. The crate is a place of comfort and warmth, but it also needs to be safe.

If your Goldendoodle proves to be a chewer, yet you still want a bed in her crate, get a tough chew version from a company that guarantees a replacement if your dog is able to chew through it at all. These beds are more costly but not nearly as costly as a trip to the emergency veterinarian. Note: even if the website or catalog shows the tough chew beds monogrammed, don't be tempted. The monogram provides a point of structural weakness your dog may be able to chew through. Also, the ad copy may say "chew proof," but until you witness it for yourself with your dog, don't believe it. Stay vigilant and check the bed for any tears or holes every time your Goldendoodle exits the crate.

Puppy Toys and Chews— Make Them Sturdy!

Puppyhood is a time of intense chewing, so you want sturdy toys. Talk to your breeder and/or veterinarian about fun toys and chews for your Goldendoodle that are appropriate for her size and age.

19

Squeaker Stress

Hate the sound of squeakers? Frustrated that almost every toy available comes with a squeaker? Is your Goldendoodle obsessed with squeaky toys? If the toy is made of cloth (do not do this with rubber toys) you can easily perform a "squeaker-ectomy." Carefully cut the threads in one of the seams near the squeaker, remove the squeaker, and then resew the seam using small, tight stitches.

Regarding dog chews, durability and vigilance are key. Avoid vegetable/grain-based chews, as they can break off in chunks and/or interfere with your dog's digestive system. A variety of natural dog chews are available, such as antlers, horns, and bully sticks. Your Goldendoodle must be supervised when she has a chew. When she gets close to the end of the chew, or you need to leave, offer her one of her favorite treats and take the chew away.

When you see any indication a toy is torn or broken, throw it away. Yes, it may mean you go through more toys, but once again, it is cheaper than a visit to the emergency veterinarian. You do not want your puppy swallowing chunks of rubber, plastic, bone, cloth, stuffing, or squeakers. These can all cause a life-threatening intestinal blockage.

Grooming Supplies

To begin, the only tools you need are a slicker brush, a double-sided comb, a nail trimmer, and a pair of safety tip scissors. As your Goldendoodle grows and her adult coat comes in, you may need to add grooming tools that better fit her coat type (see "Grooming" for more information on pages 37–41).

Outdoor Considerations

It is never wise for your Goldendoodle to be off leash in an unfenced area. Your two choices in fencing are invisible fencing or traditional fencing—chain, vinyl, or wood.

Invisible fencing is an electrified underground cable, which encircles the area designated for your Goldendoodle. She wears a special collar that emits an audible warning and then a "static correction" (a marketing euphemism for a shock) of increasing intensity as she gets closer to the invisible fence line.

To use an invisible fence successfully, you will need to diligently follow the training protocol set out by the invisible fencing company and constantly supervise your Goldendoodle while she is out in the yard.

The upside to an invisible fence is there is nothing to block your view and it can be significantly cheaper than traditional fencing. However, there are some serious concerns associated with invisible fencing. The primary drawback to invisible fencing is, while it may keep your dog in your yard, it does not keep other dogs or people out.

Using a Long Line

Until she is fairly reliable on the recall, no matter which type of fencing you choose, it's recommended you keep your Goldendoodle puppy on a long line. A long line (also known as a drag line) is a 10- to 20-foot training leash that lets you maintain some control while your puppy is in the backyard. You can hold onto the end of the long line or drop it and just let the puppy drag it around, stepping on it when you need to regain control. Stay vigilant and make sure the line does not wrap around her legs. When playing in the yard, avoid using commands and let your puppy just have fun. You need to be the most fun and interesting thing in the yard so "Catch the Puppy" does not become your puppy's favorite game. When playtime is over, simply say, "Let's Go!" and walk to the door. This should be all it takes to get your puppy to go inside with you. However, if she needs convincing, step on the long line, then entice her with a treat–never drag the puppy to you. One caveat: If your puppy needs to relieve herself in the middle of the night, it is a good idea to clip a standard leash on her and keep her in hand.

Rescues and Invisible Fencing

If you have your heart set on a rescue Goldendoodle, be aware some rescue organizations won't release a dog to a home with an invisible fence. An invisible fence cannot confine a frightened dog intent on escaping, and the shocks the dog receives during training can further traumatize a rescue. Be sure to also take into account your Goldendoodle's temperament and behavior; a fearful, nervous, or insecure dog could be traumatized by the shock they receive.

Goldendoodles are expensive, high-demand dogs, and therefore very profitable prey for dognappers. With invisible fencing, it is much easier for someone intent on dognapping your Goldendoodle to enter your property and steal your dog.

Another drawback to invisible fencing is if your Goldendoodle crosses the invisible fence line while in pursuit of something, she won't reenter the yard because of the shock she knows awaits her when she crosses the line; she may then wander off. Lastly, unless your invisible fence system has a battery backup, the invisible fence loses power if your house loses power. Your Goldendoodle might stay within its boundaries, but you do not want to take a chance; keep her on a leash when outside until power is restored.

Traditional fencing (chain, vinyl, or wood) provides the highest level of security for your Goldendoodle. It keeps her in the yard and keeps other dogs and people out. Be sure the fence is tall enough so your Goldendoodle can't leap over it. Being an athletic breed, jumping over a fence is not out of the realm of possibility, particularly if you have a standard size Goldendoodle. While a four-foot fence works for smaller Goldendoodles, it is not going to be adequate for a standard Goldendoodle; you need at least a six-foot fence. For puppies and smaller Goldendoodles, it is imperative the fence goes completely to the ground along the entire fence line and you check it frequently to make sure your dog or a local critter hasn't dug a hole under it. You'd be amazed how small a gap a puppy or small dog can wriggle through! Also, it is prudent to install an auto-close mechanism on the fence gates and, if possible, locks as well.

Create a Schedule

Have a family meeting and decide who is to be responsible for your Goldendoodle's food, water, walks, clean up, grooming, and so on, and create a schedule. Keeping a regular schedule is good for the puppy and those taking care of her. It helps everyone remember when to take her out, which prevents accidents. Keep in mind, though, the schedule is ultimately the responsibility of the adults in the home.

Find a Veterinarian

Research local veterinarians and find one *before* you bring your puppy home. Be sure to find a veterinarian offering service, care, and a philosophy you trust. Once you have found a veterinarian, make an appointment for a thorough examination for the first day or two after you bring your Goldendoodle home (for more information on finding a veterinarian, see pages 46–47).

EXPENSES? DO TELL!

Growing, growing, growing . . .

As your puppy grows, you need to purchase increasingly larger gear for her. Collars and harnesses are of particular importance. Your puppy grows *fast*!

Crate Start with a smaller crate with just enough room for your puppy to stand up and turn around. You can also purchase a larger crate and block a portion of the crate off. You want your puppy to have only enough room to spread out comfortably, otherwise she'll do her business in one end of the crate and sleep in the other.

Collars/Harnesses Pay close attention to how your puppy's collar fits; puppies outgrow their collars and harnesses very quickly. Expect to purchase three to four different sizes before your puppy reaches her final size. A word of caution: If left on all the time, a harness can create a serious matting issue.

Feeding Dishes There are two options to avoid the ends of your Goldendoodle's long ears from becoming caked with food. Purchase a narrow food dish, increasing the size as she grows. Or, she can wear a snood, which is a hood-like device designed to hold back the ears of long-eared breeds. Due to their propensity for bloat, if your Goldendoodle is a very fast eater or prone to bolting her food, purchase a special dish designed to slow down her eating speed.

Puppy K

Talk to your veterinarian about Puppy Kindergarten and ask if the disease risk in your area is low enough for your puppy to participate in this early puppy training.

Veterinarian Bills—Be Prepared!

Veterinary bills are a continuous part of pet ownership, so set aside money for regular and unexpected visits. Here are some of the expenses you can expect:

- Vaccinations
- Flea and tick preventives
- Heartworm preventives
- Wellness visits
- Spaying or neutering (if not done by your breeder or shelter)
- The dreaded run to the after-hours emergency animal hospital or veterinarian

Obedience Classes—A Must!

Enroll yourself and your puppy in an obedience class once your veterinarian clears her to attend. Obedience classes not only teach you how to train your dog, but they are also an invaluable socialization opportunity for your new Goldendoodle. Include the whole family so home training is consistent.

Be sure to ask your veterinarian, friends, and neighbors for recommendations for trainers and training facilities. You can also post a request on a neighborhood app, such as NextDoor. Once you have a list of trainers, check their websites to ascertain their certifications and training methods (look for positive, reward-based training only), and then schedule interviews and a time to watch a class in progress without your Goldendoodle (preferably one that has met for several weeks). Watch to see if the trainer keeps the class orderly and works with all the dogs and owners, not just a few obvious favorites. Do most of the puppies appear to have learned the commands? Do the owners appear confident? Is there a good rapport between the trainer and the class participants—canine and human?

Puppy Play Groups

Puppy play groups are a great way to help socialize your puppy without her getting knocked down by much larger adult dogs. Many training centers offer these play groups to their clients. Also, check with your veterinary clinic to see if they offer a puppy socialization group.

Dog Walker

Your Goldendoodle should not be confined for the entire day while you are at work. Consider having a dog walker come and let your puppy out to do her business.

Doggy Daycare

While doggy daycare is an excellent way to know your puppy is receiving attention, play, and exercise during the day, ask for recommendations. Sadly, if a daycare is poorly run, injuries and fatalities can, and have, occurred. Most doggy daycares have webcams so you can check in on your pup during the day. Make sure your veterinarian approves of the facility and has cleared your Goldendoodle to attend, based on her age and necessary vaccinations.

Books

Read as much as you can about puppies, dogs, dog behavior, and dog training. The more you know, the more confident you feel. Reading provides you with alternative methods for raising your Goldendoodle. Knowing you can try method B if method A doesn't work will keep you calmer. See the Information section on page 92 for a list of recommended books.

For the safety of your new Goldendoodle puppy and your possessions, it's very important to puppy proof your home before you bring her home. A puppy needs to learn what is acceptable to chew, and until she has learned those lessons, everything is a chew toy.

Remember, your Goldendoodle puppy is going to grow! What passes for puppy proofing today will not be adequate next week or next month. Be aware of her ever-increasing size, range, and curiosity.

If you have never owned a puppy or a dog, you may not realize how many things in your home can be hazardous to your Goldendoodle's health. The following list will help you make your home a safer place for your dog.

- ✔ Close doors or set up baby gates to rooms you don't want the puppy to get into.
- ✔ Get all plants and small pets (gerbils, guinea pigs, fish, lizards, and so on) out of puppy range.
- ✔ Get all electrical cords and curtain/shade pulls out of puppy range. Covers for electrical cords are advisable.
- ✔ Keep kids' toys picked up and out of puppy reach. Puppies do not know the difference between their toys and your child's new tablet.
- ✔ Remote controls and video game controls (which often get left on the floor) need to be put in a secure location.
- ✔ Lift up your wastebaskets. As gross as it sounds, dogs love dirty tissues and other nasty things thrown in wastebaskets. It is like having their own disgusting nose-level buffet.
- ✔ Keep a tight lid on your garbage. There are things in your garbage that can be toxic for your Goldendoodle. For example, if your dog gets into the garbage and eats the leftover chicken bones, they can do a tremendous amount of damage to your dog's digestive tract.
- ✔ Goldendoodles are notorious counter surfers! Their long legs and keen noses give them an unfair advantage when it comes to finding tasty treats on your counters—and some of those tasty treats can make them sick or even be fatal. Keep your kitchen counters clear of anything your Goldendoodle can ingest. The basket

of grapes left on the counter as an after-school snack for the kids can land your Goldendoodle in the emergency veterinary hospital with possible kidney failure. And remember, depending on how far your Goldendoodle can stretch, just placing things at the back of the counter may not be enough to stop her (see "Counter Surfing" on pages 78–79).

✔ Lock up your dirty laundry. You know that basket of stinky laundry? It smells like a buffet to your dog! It is amazing how many dogs make a snack out of dirty underwear or smelly socks. Sometimes they come out the other end . . . and sometimes they don't. When they don't, it creates a medical emergency for your dog and a financial emergency for your wallet.

✔ Check your fencing and make sure it goes completely to the ground. A puppy can flatten just like a pancake and fit through a very small gap and escape. Keep your puppy tethered or on a long line (with you in constant attendance—never leave your puppy unattended) until she is fairly reliable on the recall, even if the backyard is fenced. Check your fence line regularly for signs of digging.

✔ Lock up your yard products—fertilizers, pesticides, and herbicides are very toxic to your puppy.

✔ Keep all medications and chemicals securely locked up. A simple bottle of pain reliever consumed by a curious pup can have fatal consequences. This is important in your house, your shed, and your garage. Even if you don't think your puppy will ever be in these areas, clean them up anyway. Puppies are quick, and the last thing you want is your pup slipping out the door and into the garage and lapping up antifreeze—it is almost always fatal.

✔ Proof the bathroom! Bathrooms are another high-risk danger zone for puppies. With so many interesting smelling bottles of medications, bathroom supplies, and cleaning supplies, a puppy's curiosity can get her into a sticky situation. Keep these items up high and out of reach. And keep the lid down on the toilet. You don't want your puppy drinking from the toilet or, worse, falling in head first and drowning.

✔ Don't forget the tail. Not all puppy damage is done by puppy chewing. Make sure all breakable items are above tail level.

What's the bottom line? You must watch your puppy constantly. If you can't, put her in her crate, out of harm's way. Anything she chews and swallows, other than her food, has the potential to make her sick or, worse yet, kill her.

Your Goldendoodle
Is Finally Home!

You pick up your Goldendoodle puppy and can't wait to get her home. As exciting as this may be, make sure to ease your new puppy into her new life with you and your family.

BRINGING HOME YOUR NEW BUNDLE OF FUR

As tempting as it may be, do not transport your new Goldendoodle home on your lap. It is best to transport your new puppy in a small crate or carrier secured by a seat belt or a bungee cord. Unrestrained puppies can become projectiles if there is an accident or a sudden stomp on the brakes.

On the trip home, expect your little Goldendoodle to cry . . . a lot! She was just taken from everything she knows, so naturally she is scared and lonely. The crying will subside as she gets used to you, your family, and her new surroundings.

If you travel a distance to get your Goldendoodle, avoid rest stops. Your new puppy is not fully vaccinated and, therefore, not fully protected from various canine diseases. If you cannot avoid rest stops, bring along a supply of large puppy training pads or paper tablecloths and confine her to these when you stop.

Bring along bottled water to give your new puppy and feed her only the food the breeder fed her. Even with these precautions, chances are good your puppy will get carsick on the ride home. This is very normal, and you need not become overly concerned.

IDENTIFICATION AND TRACKING

Should she ever be lost or stolen, you will want to be able to identify and track your Goldendoodle. The following three methods of identification and tracking can help return your beloved Goldendoodle to you in the event she goes missing.

Collars

As you Goldendoodle grows, check the fit of her collar regularly. When she reaches adulthood, check her collar fit each time she is groomed—that beautiful hair has some bulk to it. The collar should be able to spin easily around her neck, yet not slip over her head.

Warning: Never use slip or choke collars. It is far too easy for a loose collar to slide off, but, more critical, if one of the end loops gets caught on something, your dog can choke to death.

Collar tags are effective identifiers; however, they can be pulled off a collar. Collars with your contact information engraved on the buckle, or an engraved nameplate attached to the collar, provide more secure identification for your Goldendoodle.

Microchips

The best and surest identification is a microchip. Your breeder may start the process by having a microchip, a rice-sized device, placed under the skin between your puppy's shoulder blades. Each microchip has a unique and unchangeable code number shelters and veterinarians can scan and read.

GPS Trackers

GPS technology now allows you to track your dog's movements from your smartphone. A GPS tracker attached to your Goldendoodle's collar lets you know, from anywhere, where your dog is. You can see if the dog walker, or your children, actually walked the dog, and for how long and how far. If your dog is lost or stolen (and the

AKC Reunite

AKC Reunite is a pet location service and a nonprofit arm of the American Kennel Club, a reliable and enduring organization. Over five million pet owners have put their trust in AKC Reunite. Some of the services offered are:

Microchip Registration

- You can register ALL the microchip numbers for ALL of the cats and dogs in your home, regardless of the microchip company of origin.
- Create a profile for each pet, including a current photo.
- Update the profile and photo as needed.
- You now have an online repository of critical information for all of your furry friends.

Lost Pet Alert

Call, e-mail, or log-in to report your missing animal and the date, time, and location where your pet was last seen.

Using your pet's profile and last seen information, the AKC Reunite system creates a PDF of a Lost Pet Alert flyer, and then broadcasts it to participating animal shelters, veterinarians, and pet lovers in the area your pet was last seen—anywhere in the country.

Using the PDF of the Lost Pet Alert flyer, you can print flyers, either at home or at a local copy center, and distribute them in the area where your pet was lost. When your pet is found, AKC Reunite contacts you with her location. For more information, visit their website: *www.akcreunite.org*.

thieves do not remove the tracker) you can locate and track your dog. There is the initial cost of the tracker and base station, and then a monthly service fee.

WHAT'S IN A NAME?

Your new Goldendoodle needs an identity all her own. Give her a fairly simple name, preferably no longer than two syllables, so she recognizes it easily. Use her name often, but only in a happy tone. Eventually she'll recognize the sounds you make as her name. Practice often, and every time she looks at you, reward her with a treat and/or warm, effusive praise. Never use her name when

reprimanding her. When training, her name is used frequently; you want only positive associations with it. Also, make sure to use only her single name when training. For example, "sweet silly, willy, Lilly" becomes just plain "Lilly" or "Lil" when training.

ACCLIMATING YOUR PUPPY TO YOUR HOME

Puppies Need Rest

Like babies, young puppies need a lot of sleep to develop properly, both physically and emotionally. During her first week with you, resist the temptation to take her to visit

Introducing Your Puppy to Other Pets

Keep all of your noncanine pets, such as rodents or reptiles, away from the puppy. If introductions must be made, with the family cat for example, have the puppy leashed during the first several encounters. (An excellent article on puppy/cat introductions is listed in the Information section on page 92.) As she matures, her hunting instincts come into play during her interactions. This can lead her to suddenly chase the cat she has snuggled with or ignored up until this point. Until she reaches maturity and her behavior is reliable, keep a close eye on her interactions with other species.

friends and family or to have a parade of visitors into your home. Let her settle in and get to know you and your family—her new pack. Even if she seems fine and at ease (tail wagging nonstop, eating and eliminating on schedule), coming to a new home is intensely stressful for a young puppy.

Introducing Your Puppy to the Rest of the Pack

Before you bring your new Goldendoodle puppy home, make sure your existing dogs are current with all of their vaccinations. If you have more than one dog, introduce them to the puppy one at a time. Now, although they seem to get along, wait a couple of weeks before you leave the puppy and your other dogs alone together. Puppies respect the adult dogs in a home because they set the rules from the moment the puppy arrives. As the puppy grows, be aware of her size change in relation to your other dogs; if there is a large disparity in sizes, play must be closely supervised.

Where Should My New Puppy Sleep?

Although you might not want her crate to be in your bedroom long term, placing the crate next to your bed for her first few nights is a good idea. The use of the crate is an important part of housetraining and having the crate next to the bed allows you to hear her if she begins to stir and needs to go outside during the night. Once she feels secure and sleeps more restfully during the night, you can move the crate to another part of the house.

Let Your Puppy Get Settled and Be Cautious!

Again, give your new Goldendoodle puppy a good solid week to acclimate to you and your family before friends come to visit. When friends do come, have them remove their shoes and leave them outside. Canine diseases are unwittingly picked up and transported directly into your home on the bottom of shoes.

FEEDING YOUR PUPPY

Feeding Schedule

Feed your Goldendoodle at the same times each day so your puppy develops a routine and an internal schedule.

Between eight and sixteen weeks: Feed your puppy three meals per day.

From sixteen weeks on: Keep your Goldendoodle on a feeding schedule of two meals per day.

Note: The exception is a Goldendoodle whose lineage has a history of bloat. All

puppies in that line are at greater risk for bloat and should be fed three to four small meals a day for their entire lives.

What Type of Food to Feed

It is critical you discuss your Goldendoodle's nutritional needs with your veterinarian and her breeder. There is a myriad of diet options for your Goldendoodle: traditional kibble, grain-free kibble, freeze-dried raw food, frozen raw food, home-cooked food, home-prepared raw food, and the list goes on. Go with the highest quality food your budget allows. Just like humans, the quality of your Goldendoodle's diet directly impacts her health and well-being.

The canine digestive system is very sensitive to dietary changes, so continue to feed your puppy the same food she had at the breeder. If you want to change her food, do it very gradually by mixing the foods with increasing increments of the new food, matched by decreasing increments of the old food. Watch your puppy and her stools carefully during this transition to make sure the new food is not causing any irritations to her digestive system.

Start with a 3:1 ratio (¾ old food, ¼ new food) for three to four days. If she tolerates this well, change to a 1:1 ratio (½ old food, ½ new food) for another three to four days. If she adjusts to this without any issues, move to a 1:3 ratio (¼ old food, ¾ new food) for three to four days. If there are no changes in her stools, change her over to 100 percent new food, and again watch her for three to four days for any stool issues. Yes, it can take two weeks to change a dog's food—be patient. A lack of patience with the process can have an unpleasant outcome—all over your carpet.

How Much Should I Feed?

The type of food you feed makes a difference. The higher the quality, the less you need to feed your puppy. It is better to keep your Goldendoodle on the lean side. As with humans, obesity in dogs causes a myriad of health issues.

Have a conversation with your breeder and your veterinarian on this subject, particularly if your Goldendoodle has the potential to be a large dog. It is very important to feed large dog puppies carefully to control their growth; accelerated growth can result in bone deformities or weakness.

PREVENTING NIPPING AND MOUTHING

The first order of business when training your Goldendoodle puppy is to inhibit the nipping reflex. This is called bite inhibition. Your Goldendoodle puppy would normally learn her bite inhibition from her mother and littermates. However, since puppies are taken away from their mothers at a young age, it is up to her human family to teach her not to nip.

One great way to inhibit the nipping reflex is to allow your Goldendoodle puppy to play and socialize with other puppies and well-socialized older dogs. If your puppy becomes too rough while playing, the other puppy may give out a very loud, sharp cry. It's through this type of socialization your puppy learns to control her nipping reflex.

Stop Nipping Me!

By taking advantage of your Goldendoodle's retriever instincts, it's relatively simple to teach your puppy bite inhibition. If your puppy wants attention from you, put a toy in her mouth before you begin to pet and touch her. If the toy is dropped, the petting stops.

Who Knew Puppy Teeth Were So Sharp?

Nipping and mouthing are normal social activities for young puppies when playing with their littermates, and your Goldendoodle puppy will naturally extend this behavior to her new pack members—you and your family. Unlike adult canine teeth, puppy teeth are needle fine and extremely sharp. It is important to teach your puppy what is appropriate when it comes to using her sharp teeth.

Hands to Yourself!

Never hit or slap your puppy—never, ever. Why? Physically reprimanding your puppy won't stop her from nipping; it will simply scare and confuse her. Physical punishment is the surest way to erode the trust and respect that forms the basis of an effective training program and a healthy lifelong relationship with your dog.

If she does nip, tell her *"No nip,"* put her in a *sit*, wait four seconds, and then reward the *sit* with either a toy in the mouth or a treat. (See "How-To: Children and Puppies" on pages 42–43 for information on teaching children how to handle a nipping puppy.)

My Puppy Is Chewing Everything!

Puppies need to be taught what they can and cannot chew. If you find your Goldendoodle puppy with something she shouldn't be chewing on, simply tell her *"No,"* take the item away, put her in a *sit*, wait four seconds, and then reward the *sit* with a toy she can chew.

Puppy Toys

Puppy toys must be durable. If you notice a toy is ripped, shredded, or missing a chunk, try to locate all the pieces. If there are pieces and parts that cannot be found or accounted for, keep a close eye on your puppy and her stool. Look for any changes in her behavior or the texture and/or frequency of her stools.

As your puppy grows, her size dictates the size and durability of her toys. A mini-Goldendoodle naturally has a less forceful bite than a large standard Goldendoodle. That said, chewing and shredding toys is a lot of fun for dogs and puppies of any size, so stay aware.

PLAYTIME

Playtime is an exciting time for your Goldendoodle puppy, not to mention fun for you, too. Keep playtime fun and short and end it before your puppy gets too tired. At their core, Goldendoodles are retrievers, and some will retrieve to the point of exhaustion. You do not want to let playtime get to this point.

Appropriate vs. Inappropriate Games to Play

Goldendoodles are joyful, eager to please, and always ready to participate in a game. Puppies learn a tremendous amount from play, particularly when you incorporate some of their formal training. However, some caution needs to be employed when playing with your Goldendoodle, as certain games, although loads of fun for both humans and

canines, can teach your puppy the wrong lessons.

Tug-of-war and wrestling seem like relatively harmless and natural games, don't they? Unfortunately, these innocent games can send all the wrong messages to your puppy. Never, ever wrestle with your puppy or dog. This outwardly innocent interaction can produce feelings of rivalry and aggression, easily escalating to potentially dangerous situations later in your dog's life.

Tug-of-war is fine, but with a caveat. It is suggested you let the puppy win every other time to help build her confidence; however, you need to teach her "*Out/Give/Drop*" so she relinquishes her side of the tug on command (see pages 76–77 for instructions on teaching this command). Here is the caveat: never play tug-of-war with a dog who places a high value on an item and/or shows tendencies for resource guarding. These behaviors can easily escalate into potentially dangerous situations.

Another game to avoid is chase. Playing chase teaches your puppy it is acceptable to run after and jump on people. In addition, she learns running away from you is fun, which is in direct opposition to her recall training.

Fetch, searching for hidden toys or searching for you, and simple tricks are stimulating games for your puppy. Again, teach her "*Out/ Give/Drop*" so she relinquishes the retrieved item on command.

EXERCISE AND ACTIVITIES

Your Goldendoodle needs exercise. How you exercise your puppy during her first year as she experiences rapid bone growth makes a difference in the long-term health of your

dog's hips and/or elbows. Goldendoodles can be genetically predisposed to both elbow and hip dysplasia (yet another reason to make sure your puppy's lineage is thoroughly tested and cleared). Too much hard exercise, too early in life, can cause long-term joint issues for your dog. Moderate exercise combined with a lot of play is the perfect mix to keep your puppy happy and healthy.

Swimming

Descendants from water dogs, Goldendoodles are enthusiast swimmers. Swimming provides terrific non-weight-bearing exercise. Naturally, you need to be cautious about where you allow your Goldendoodle to swim. If you won't swim in the water, neither should your dog. Your Goldendoodle should always wear a flotation vest with a handle on top when swimming—dogs can drown just as easily as people.

When she is finished swimming, rinse her with fresh water, and then pat her coat with a thick towel. Brush her thoroughly when she is dry, and clean her ears with a medicated ear cleaner.

Walking

Sidewalks and roads are hard surfaces, and dogs under the age of twelve months should not exercise on these surfaces for long periods. The jarring force experienced when walking or running on a hard surface can, over time, have a negative impact on bones and joints.

If your Goldendoodle is under twelve months of age, she should not engage in strenuous, forced exercise, such as jogging or walking for several miles on a leash. Too much leash walking too early on can cause loose ligaments and fragile joints, aggravating hips and/or elbow joints.

Outdoor Walks

Until she is fully immunized, your puppy is not ready for walks outdoors where other dogs have relieved themselves. Leash train and walk your dog in your yard. It is critical to keep her within the safety of your own property until she is fully vaccinated.

Off-leash Running

Your Goldendoodle also needs to free run in a fenced area to fully develop the muscles supporting her hips. Just walking, which is a singular, forward motion, robs your Goldendoodle of the lateral motion essential for healthy hips. This is particularly critical if your puppy or dog is diagnosed with chronic hip dysplasia (CHD), because the defective hip joints need all the muscle support they can get.

Beware the Stairs!

It can be fun to watch your puppy race up and down the stairs, but this is an unnatural angle for her developing hips and should be avoided. Use gates to keep your puppy away from the stairs and carry her up or down for as long as you are physically able. If you have wood stairs, carpet treads give puppies and older dogs more traction and prevent slipping. Keeping her paw pad hair trimmed also gives her better traction on both stairs and hard surface floors.

Observe your Goldendoodle puppy closely to make sure her playtime, daily routine, and exercise do not consist of jumping off high

Is My Puppy Possessed? No! It's the Zoomies!

Suddenly, one day, your darling Goldendoodle puppy acts like she's possessed. She is running in circles at top speed, stopping occasionally to look at you with wild eyes, giving you a sharp bark, and then returning to the wild paced, circular running. Stay calm—your pup is not crazy. Your puppy has the "zoomies" (also called "puppy crazies"). Just sit back and enjoy the show. Don't be surprised if this is a daily event that lasts for about five to ten minutes. It is perfectly normal canine behavior; however, it can be the result of a buildup of puppy energy. Take a look at her exercise schedule to determine if she is getting enough exercise in her day.

objects. Something as simple as jumping off the sofa or the bed can, over time, have a negative effect on her joints. If she is allowed on furniture, invest in some pet steps so she isn't leaping off and landing hard on her front legs. Sliding or slipping on smooth surfaces is also a potential danger to your Goldendoodle. If you have hard surfaces in your home, consider strategically placing area rugs and carpets so your puppy or dog has nonskid surfaces to navigate your home.

GROOMING

Whether you groom your Goldendoodle at home or take her to a professional groomer, it is important that your Goldendoodle get used to people handling her. If you opt to have your Goldendoodle professionally groomed, be sure you give her a good all-over check at least once a month. Run your hands over her entire body, examine her pads and her teeth and gums, check her eyes, inspect her ears, and (yuck!) lift her tail and check her anus. It is important to know what "normal" looks and feels like for your Goldendoodle so when something abnormal appears, you can recognize it and do something about it.

Grooming at Home—Regular Maintenance

Unless she rolled in something disgusting, your Goldendoodle does not need to be bathed frequently. She may only need to be bathed once a month, or every other month if she's not very active. If she is muddy, let the mud dry, and then brush her. When you do bathe her, look for shampoos designed to not strip the coat and skin of its natural oils.

If you intend to groom your Goldendoodle at home, do it on a raised surface, preferably on an actual grooming table. This gives better access to all areas of her body and it is much easier on your back and knees. Be sure there is enough room for your Goldendoodle to lie down.

Until you are confident your Goldendoodle will not jump off the table or try to run away from you (some dogs don't like to be brushed), keep a collar and leash on her.

Hair

Depending on her coat type, your Goldendoodle's coat can be high maintenance. The curlier and softer the coat, the more prone it is to matting and the more dif-

ficult it is to brush out. Some Goldendoodles need brushing every few days, others every few weeks. You'll determine on your own how often you need to brush your Goldendoodle and how often she needs professional grooming. If your dog's coat tends to fluff after brushing, spritz a little water on the coat to calm it down.

It is best to brush in sections, working each section thoroughly to remove any mats. Begin with the slicker brush, and brush in short, firm strokes against the lay of the fur. Then, using the wider side, comb each layer of hair in the direction it grows, and then repeat with the fine side of the comb. To avoid mats, make sure you get right down to the skin.

Mats

Your Goldendoodle's hair can easily tangle, especially when she is a puppy, and form hard bundles of fur known as mats. Brushing your dog's hair thoroughly every week produces fewer mats than brushing more often but not as thoroughly. Spraying the mat with a conditioning lotion first can loosen the mat and make it easier to remove.

Brush out any mats before bathing your puppy. Bathing makes mats harder and tighter, and brushing them out post-bath is nearly impossible.

Keeping your dog mat-free is an ongoing battle for most Goldendoodle owners, especially when the Goldendoodle is young. Your Goldendoodle's puppy coat will transition to an adult coat somewhere between nine and twelve months. During this time, you can look forward to some shedding even if your

Goldendoodle has a nonshedding coat, so plan to brush your Goldendoodle every few days during this transition period. Even with diligence, the fine puppy coat often becomes matted. This is the time most Goldendoodles get their first close clip or shave. The benefit of shaving her at this point is the adult coat can grow in without the puppy coat, and your Goldendoodle gets a fresh start.

Trimming Your Goldendoodle

A good time to trim your Goldendoodle is when her hair is fluffy from brushing. Trim the hair around the collar and neck, on the ear flap near the cheek, under the elbows, around the paws, and between the paw pads, and give a sanitary trim around the elimination areas (see "Instructions for Your Groomer" on page 41).

If your Goldendoodle is prone to ear infections, shaving close to the skin on her neck and under her ears allows for better airflow into the ears, which keeps the ears dryer.

It is important for your Goldendoodle to be able to see her world clearly, so trim the hair around her eyes to keep them free of obstruction. This is likely the first trim you will do and the one you will do most frequently.

Ears

One of the reasons people love Goldendoodles is because they have long, floppy ears. However, the floppy ear structure also means they are prone to ear infections due to restricted airflow into the ear canal. Additionally, with the Golden Retriever tendency for waxy, dirty ears and the Poodle tendency for very hairy ear canals,

Goldendoodles are vulnerable to ear problems. Cleaning with a medicated ear wash once a week keeps the ears free of waxy buildup and in great condition to hear her favorite word, "treat." If your dog has very hairy ear canals or is susceptible to ear infections, it may be necessary to pluck the hair in the ear canal. Have a veterinary technician or a professional groomer show you the proper way to pluck the ear hair or have him/her do it for you.

To safely clean deep inside the ear, use cotton gauze soaked in either a medicated cleaning solution recommended by your veterinarian or a solution of 40 percent white vinegar and 60 percent distilled water. Do not use cotton swabs in your Goldendoodle's ear. A dog's ear is L-shaped, so while a cotton swab won't harm the ear drum, there is a real danger of packing the ear debris farther down into the ear canal and into the inaccessible lower portion of the L-shape.

If you are unsure of how deep to clean inside of your Goldendoodle's ear canal, have your veterinary technician give you a lesson in ear cleaning during your next visit.

Dental Care

There is a selection of canine dental supplies at the pet store to maintain the health of your puppy's teeth. To keep them pearly white, start brushing your Goldendoodle's teeth, once or twice a week, as early as possible.

Most veterinarians show you how to brush your puppy's teeth during your initial wellness visit. If this is not part of the wellness visit, make an appointment with one of the veterinary technicians for a quick lesson.

Warning: Do not use human toothpaste; it is made to be spat out. Dogs swallow their toothpaste, so it must be edible and designed for dogs.

Paws

If you hear a "click, click" when your Goldendoodle walks across a hard surface, it is time to trim her nails. Nails need to be trimmed every six to ten weeks. Keeping your Goldendoodle's nails trimmed to a correct and comfortable length is important to her long-term health.

Begin trimming your puppy's nails when she is very young. This often consists of just nipping the sharp tip off of the nail. Get your puppy used to her feet being handled and hearing the sound of the nail clipper or a Dremel tool.

Use caution when clipping her nails. A dog's nail has a live center, known as the quick, that bleeds and causes your Goldendoodle pain if clipped. If your dog has lighter colored nails, the quick is clearly visible and easy to avoid. If your Goldendoodle has black nails, look on the underside of the nail to try and discern where the quick ends. Have your veterinarian or the veterinary technician show you how to trim your Goldendoodle's nails, particularly if her nails are black and the quick is not visible. If you are not comfortable trimming her nails, bring her to the groomer or the veterinary office for a trim.

Make sure to trim the hair that grows between her paw pads. Long paw pad hair not only causes your Goldendoodle to slip and fall on smooth surfaces or stairs, but it is also a magnet for dirt, burrs, and snow.

Caution: Beware of hot pavement in the summer. Either walk your Goldendoodle on the grass or early in the morning before the sidewalks heat up. Conversely, watch for salt, ice melt chemicals, and snow buildup between her paw pads in the winter. Acquire dog boots for your Goldendoodle to help prevent this.

Going to the Groomer

If you choose to take your puppy to the groomer, be sure your groomer knows this is a Goldendoodle, not a Poodle, or you could be in for a surprise. To be on the safe side, give the groomer specific instructions (see "Instructions for Your Groomer" on this page). If you have a picture of what you want the final outcome to look like, bring it along.

If trips to the groomer are going to be a regular part of your Goldendoodle's life, start taking her early in life so she can get used to the noise and commotion of a grooming salon. When she is young she probably won't need a coat trim, so simply take her in for a bath, brush, ear cleaning, and nail trim.

How to Choose a Groomer

As with choosing a veterinarian, groomers are best found through referrals. If you see someone in your neighborhood with a Goldendoodle or a Labradoodle whose cut you like, ask him/her who does the dog's grooming. If you can't get a referral, ask the groomers in your area if they can provide ref-

Instructions for Your Groomer

The best instructions for grooming Goldendoodles are found on the IDOG Rescue and Rehome website at *www.idogrescue.com*. Simply go to "Resources," then "Grooming Guide," and then click on the "Professional Doodle Grooming Guide." This brings you to a two-page PDF of precise instructions you can print. Along with detailed photos, there are also boxes in each section to check off your particular preferences regarding the length of trim for each body part. This is an excellent tool if you take your Goldendoodle to a groomer, as well as a fantastic guide for home grooming. While you are on the site, check out the Doodle dogs available for adoption!

erences from Goldendoodle or Labradoodle owners. (Labradoodles are trimmed in the same manner as Goldendoodles.)

It is important to prepare your children for life with a puppy by teaching them the proper way to interact with her. This means setting boundaries on child/puppy activities and interactions. If you teach your children the correct way to treat the puppy from the

beginning, life with your Goldendoodle will be rewarding. Until your puppy reaches maturity, you must supervise all interactions between your child and your Goldendoodle. If an adult is unable to supervise, it is best to put the puppy in her crate.

Young Puppies Will Nip

Until they are taught not to, it is very natural for young puppies to nip; it is how they interact with their littermates. This can be painful and very disconcerting for children who may think the puppy is being mean or wants to hurt them. Explain to your children that puppies naturally nip their littermates when playing and your new Goldendoodle is not trying to hurt them—she's just trying to play.

It is important to teach your children how to behave when your puppy inevitably nips them. You will make life less stressful for everyone by preparing them for a nipping puppy and practicing what to do before the arrival of your new Goldendoodle.

When a puppy nips, all play must stop immediately. The puppy is already in a state of excitement, so it is important the children avoid any high-pitch screaming. This is difficult, particularly if a child just experienced the nip of razor-sharp puppy teeth, but this is where practice and preparation pay huge dividends. Have your child stand tall like a tree and at the same time tell the puppy, "*No nipping!*" in a low, firm, authoritative voice. Then, have your child turn away from the puppy and put his/her hands out of the puppy's reach (on top of the head, under the armpits, and so on).

As the puppy moves to face your child, make sure your child continues to move so his/her back is toward the puppy. At this point, if the puppy calms down, praise them both quietly and let them continue to play. If the puppy is still in an excited state, it might be a good time for her to have a little quiet time in her crate or go for a walk to get rid of some puppy energy.

Picking Up the Puppy

Children often want to pick up their new Goldendoodle puppies and carry them around as if they are dolls. Children should not pick up puppies unless there is an adult present. A puppy is naturally wiggly, and a child can easily drop and injure the puppy or the puppy can squirm away and be injured.

Have your child sit, preferably on the floor rather than on an elevated surface, such as a chair, and put the puppy in the child's lap. To help the puppy relax and settle down, have your child give the puppy a chew toy. A young teething puppy chews on everything, including the young arms and hands of the child holding her. A chew toy gives her something besides your child to gnaw on, and it keeps her content in your child's lap for a longer period of time.

Children and Puppy Snacks

All parents are proud when their children finally learn the concept of sharing, but when you add a puppy to your family, all the rules about sharing change. Children must understand if they share their snacks with the puppy, it could make the puppy very sick, or worse, be fatal. You can avoid this by having a special plastic jar of treats the children can give to the puppy. Explain to your child that puppies can get a bellyache from too many treats just like he/she can.

Helping Care for the Puppy

Give children some responsibility for puppy care; however, you should not expect them to be solely responsible. Always supervise them to make sure the task is done and completed correctly.

With your help, young children can carry out simple tasks such as feeding the puppy at certain times or filling a water bowl.

Make a chart for your children to put a sticker on every time they complete their assigned task. This makes it fun for them, and you can easily see whether their tasks are complete for the day. Just be sure they are completed properly.

Health and Wellness

Any discussion on the subject of Goldendoodle health needs to start with the health of the sire (the male parent dog) and dam (the female parent dog), as well as the preceding generations.

YOUR PUPPY'S PARENTS

Any discussion on the subject of Goldendoodle health needs to start with the health of the sire (the male parent dog) and dam (the female parent dog), as well as the preceding generations. The parent breeds of the Goldendoodle share many genetic defects that all breeding dogs must be cleared of before they are bred.

Hip Dysplasia

Golden Retrievers and Standard Poodles share a common and critical health concern—hip dysplasia. Canine Hip Dysplasia (CHD) is a structural abnormality of the hips, which causes the ball at the top of the thigh bone to wear against, rather than slide within, the socket joint in the pelvis. This wear creates a painful osteoarthritis in the hip joints. Surgery can often correct the problem, but it can be extensive, expensive, and painful. While CHD is a hereditary disease, it can be exacerbated by rapid growth, poor diet, and exercise too vigorous for young developing hips.

A responsible breeder screens his/her breeding dogs for hip dysplasia and only breeds dogs whose hip scores indicate healthy hips. A final and definitive score cannot be obtained until the dog is two years of age; therefore, the dog should not be bred *before* two years of age.

Currently, the only way to detect CHD is with an X-ray. The following organizations are the most commonly used to read and certify the X-rays.

OFA The Orthopedic Foundation for Animals (USA) assigns a rating of: Normal ("Excellent," "Good," "Fair"), "Borderline," and Dysplastic ("Mild," "Moderate," "Severe"). The official score can only be obtained from tests run after the dog is two years old. Prior to two years of age, the OFA scores are considered "preliminary."

PennHIP The University of Pennsylvania Hip Improvement Project (USA/Australia) uses three different views of the hips (Compression, Distraction, and Hip Extended) to assess, measure, and interpret the laxity (looseness) of the hip joint. The earliest a dog can be PennHIP screened is four months of age.

BVA The British Veterinary Association (UK/Australia) assigns a number to each hip, with the score being the sum of the two hips.

When looking at the hip scores of the sire and dams, here are some guidelines as to where the scores should fall:

OFA: Good or Excellent.

PennHIP: .44–.55 is average. Dogs with scores of .6–.7 or higher should not be bred.

BVA: Should be 13 or less. Dogs with scores over 16 should not be bred.

Be cautious of anyone who tells you his/her breeding dogs' test scores are "pending." The use of this term indicates they bred prior to testing and it should be considered a warning sign.

Other Parental Health Issues

Eyes The eyes of the Goldendoodle parents must be tested annually. A painless examination is performed each year by a veterinarian certified by the American College of Veterinary Ophthalmologists. The results are registered with OFA's Eye Certification

Registry. If a breeder tells you this eye test, also known as a CERF test, is a one-and-done test—walk away. This test must be done annually and may not be accurate if done before the age of two.

Progressive Retinal Atrophy (PRA) is an inheritable eye disease. The Golden Retriever and the Poodle both can carry the same mutated gene that causes PRA. PRA refers to a group of diseases that cause the retina of the eye to degenerate. Depending on the type of PRA, this can happen slowly over time (Slow Progression PRA) or very quickly (Rapid Progression PRA). In either case, the result is declining vision and eventual blindness. The mode of inheritance for PRA is, in most cases, an autosomal recessive gene, requiring both parent dogs to carry the gene for the disease to be passed on to their young. DNA testing identifies dogs who carry the gene for three versions of PRA: *prcd*-PRA, which is present in Poodles, Golden Retrievers, and Goldendoodles; and GR-PRA1 and GR-PRA2, which are only present in Golden Retrievers and Goldendoodles.

von Willebrand Disease (vWD) is an inherited bleeding disorder common in Poodles and, to a lesser degree, Golden Retrievers. It is similar in nature to the human bleeding disorder hemophilia.

The mode of inheritance for vWD is an autosomal dominant gene, requiring only one parent dog to carry the gene for the disease to be passed on to their young. Testing for vWD is done by measuring the von Willebrand's factor in a blood sample or, in the case of the Poodle parent, by checking the DNA.

The parents of your Goldendoodle should both be cleared of this bleeding disorder before breeding.

Elbow Dysplasia Elbow dysplasia is a concern in both Poodles and Golden Retrievers. Elbow dysplasia, like hip dysplasia, is a polygenic condition, meaning an unknown number of genes control the polygenic condition; however, the expression of those genes can be influenced by several factors, including breed, rate of growth, nutrition, exercise, and gender. The Orthopedic Foundation for Animals (OFA) offers a scoring system and database for elbow dysplasia.

Patellas (Knee Caps) The patellas protect the front of the stifle joints on the rear legs and slide into grooves in the femurs. When the groove is too shallow, the patella slips to either the inside of the knee (medial luxation) or the outside of the knee (lateral luxation). The testing and clearance for patellas is only required on Miniature/Toy Poodle parents and Mini/Medium Goldendoodle parents.

For more information on health clearances from the Goldendoodle Association of North America (GANA), see Information section, page 91.

YOUR PUPPY'S HEALTH

Locate a Veterinarian and Schedule an Appointment

Before you bring your puppy home, locate both a regular *and* an emergency veterinarian. Keep the phone numbers and hours for both clinics posted where they can be quickly found in an emergency. (Many clinics provide magnets with their contact information you can put on your refrigerator.)

If you do not already have a veterinarian you trust, ask friends, neighbors, relatives, and strangers. (Just kidding! Sort of . . . taking a trip to a local dog park and asking some of the dog owners there for veterinarian recommendations may lead you to a good veterinarian.) A call to a local animal shelter or rescue organization may also get you a few names worth checking out.

If you are a first-time pet owner, it is a good idea to visit the veterinarian clinic before you bring your new puppy in for her first visit. It helps to meet the veterinarian and his/her staff, as well as to be able to hear what an active clinic sounds like. The noises distressed animals make can be very disconcerting. It helps your puppy immensely if you stay calm during her first veterinarian visit and knowing what to expect goes a long way toward being able to relax.

Your veterinarian and clinic staff are your partners in caring for your Goldendoodle. Always feel free to ask them any questions or share any concerns you may have regarding your Goldendoodle's health.

Schedule a preliminary examination with your veterinarian for your new puppy. You will also need to schedule follow-up visits to complete your puppy's vaccinations.

The First Wellness Visit

Schedule a wellness visit with your veterinarian within the first two days of bringing your puppy home. Bring along the vaccination and deworming schedule your breeder gave you. This helps your

Questions to Ask Your Potential Veterinarian

1. How long is the wait for a regular (nonemergency) appointment?
2. How available are you for emergencies?
3. How many years have you been in the community?
4. How many veterinarians, veterinary nurses, and veterinary technicians do you have?
5. Do you have a specialty?
   Some clinics are geared toward general practice, while others specialize in surgical procedures, cats, exotics, and so on. Make sure dogs make up the bulk of the practice.

Be Clear and Concise

If your dog is ill, take a video with your smartphone of the behavior and/or symptoms. A veterinarian gains valuable insight by seeing and hearing what you are experiencing at home, as dogs often don't display the behavior/symptoms in the veterinary office.

Clear and concise information regarding your Goldendoodle and her health is critical to your veterinarian, particularly in an emergency situation. In addition to the video, create a list of symptoms and observations along with questions before you get to the clinic.

veterinarian determine what vaccinations your pup needs and when best to administer them. The veterinarian will also want a stool sample, so be prepared.

Until your puppy is fully vaccinated at 16 weeks, keep her in your lap or in a travel crate—NO paws on the floor at the veterinary office! Without the full complement of their vaccinations, puppies are vulnerable to disease and need to be protected. Remember, this is the place where people bring their sick animals, and even the cleanest of clinics do not disinfect their floors between every patient. So, carry (or crate) your puppy, but keep her on a leash in case she twists away from you.

During your puppy's first visit, the veterinary technician will get some basic information about your puppy, give her a look over, ooh and ah, take her temperature,

and then take the stool sample to the lab for analysis. The veterinarian then comes in and gives your puppy a thorough examination, her next round of shots, and worming medication. The veterinarian may ask you to restrain your dog for her exam. Some veterinary clinics take your puppy into their "staff only" area to administer shots or to draw blood. The reason behind this is so the owner's anxiety isn't conveyed to the puppy and there are other experienced staff members available to help.

DEWORMING AND VACCINATIONS

Deworming

Your breeder will do the preliminary deworming. Deworming begins at two weeks and is repeated at four, six, and eight weeks of age. Worms are discussed in more detail on page 54.

Vaccinations

Your puppy should receive her first round of core vaccines at six to eight weeks of age, before you bring her home. The three preventable diseases, which are considered core vaccines, are Parvovirus, Canine Distemper, and Infectious Canine Hepatitis.

Noncore vaccines are often dependent upon where you live and your dog's lifestyle. They include leptospirosis, canine parainfluenza and *Bordetella bronchiseptica* (both are causes of "kennel cough" and the vaccine is given twice per year via a nasal mist), and *Borrelia burgdorferi* (Lyme disease). Consult with your veterinarian to select the proper vaccines for your Goldendoodle.

Rabies vaccines are required by law and the frequency is dictated by local regulations. Discuss the risk of reactions and side effects from vaccinations with your veterinarian.

SPAY AND NEUTER

Spaying and neutering not only prevent unwanted puppies, but also help prevent certain adult afflictions, including pyometra (an abscessed, infected uterus) and mammary cancer in females, and reduces the risk of diabetes in males. There are also behavioral benefits, as neutered males are less likely to be aggressive.

Generally, spay and neuter are done around the age of six months, before dogs reach sexual maturity, but can be done as early as six to twelve weeks of age (pediatric spay/neuter). Some Goldendoodle breeders spay/neuter their puppies before they go to their new owners. This is a positive step that prevents dishonest people from using these puppies as part of their puppy mill or back-yard breeding business. However, there are some potential drawbacks to a spay/neuter before dogs reach full maturity. It can cause spay incontinence in some female dogs. Also, because the sexual hormones interact with the growth hormones, physical differences can occur in dogs neutered before reaching sexual maturity, as they often have longer legs, flatter chests, and narrower skulls. These differences put added stress on the joints and cause problems for active dogs as they age, particularly dogs who participate in agility sports.

There is also the belief you should wait until dogs reach sexual maturity and com-

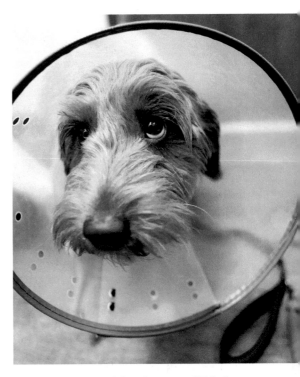

plete their physical development. With these varied schools of thought regarding the optimal time to spay/neuter a puppy, and the need to balance potential health risks and benefits, it is best to discuss this in detail with your veterinarian and make an informed decision on what is best for you and your Goldendoodle. See the Information section on page 91 for a study of the effects of early spay/neuter in Golden Retrievers.

THINGS TO CHECK REGULARLY

The purpose of regular checks is threefold. First, you must know what is normal for your Goldendoodle so you can recognize changes. Second, because dogs hide any weaknesses, you may not know there is a problem if you are not tuned into your Goldendoodle and her body. Third, regular checks of your puppy desensitize her to being touched, making it easier for you and your veterinarian to treat her when medical attention is required.

Those Big Floppy Ears

As mentioned in the Grooming section of Chapter 3, Goldendoodles have heavy ear flaps that restrict air flow into their ear canals, thus trapping moisture. This makes them prone to fungal ear infections. Woolly ears can also increase the risk of fungal and bacterial infections, while allergies can cause bilateral ear infections (see "Allergies" on pages 58–59).

If you notice a foul smell emanating from your dog, it is likely a yeasty ear infection or cankers caused by ear mites. These problems become more common when wax and dirt mix with inner ear hair. Check inside her ears, and if you see a buildup of dirt, clean the ears. Once the ears are clean, check the color of the skin inside the ear; if it is red and looks inflamed, your Goldendoodle more than likely has an ear infection and needs to go to the veterinarian.

Eyes

Your puppy's eyes should be clear and have a normal level of discharge. If your puppy starts to have large amounts of discharge or her eyes look bloodshot, there may be a problem. See your veterinarian.

Mouth

Check your puppy's teeth and gums regularly. Her teeth should be nice and white without any plaque buildup. Plaque builds up near the gum line, so look carefully. If you see plaque developing, consult your veterinarian. Plaque can cause dental issues that can have detrimental, long-term health effects for your Goldendoodle.

Your Goldendoodle's gums should be a nice shade of pink. Bright red, blue, or very pale to white gums should be brought to the attention of your veterinarian immediately, as each are indicative of a potentially life-threatening situation.

Paws and Pads

Check your puppy's nails and pads frequently to ensure they are in good order. Keep your pup's nails trimmed, as well as the fur between the pads.

Skin

Do an overall check of her skin, looking/feeling for bumps and parasites like ticks and fleas. If you find a lump or bump, make note of its location and have it checked by your veterinarian, particularly if it seems to be growing fast.

BODILY FUNCTIONS

Dog owners become keen observers of canine bodily functions and the resulting outputs. And if that isn't enough, they discuss these outputs, in detail, with other dog owners and consider it a perfectly normal topic of conversation. At this point, you know beyond the shadow of a doubt that you have become a bona fide dog person.

The Back End

It has been said, "poo is the window to your dog's health," and the longer you live with dogs, the truer it becomes. Very often when you call the veterinarian about your dog, it is because you noticed a change in the texture, frequency, or urgency of her bowel movements. And yes, of course, you have to bring in a sample. So, let's get into this less than pleasant, yet vital, topic.

Stools Your dog's stools should be firm, well-formed, and consistent in shape and color, entering the world without undo effort. This is a sign of well-digested food. You will learn what is "normal" for your dog and will notice when things change. Although most dogs have the occasional soft stool, it becomes a concern if it persists for several days. Soft and unformed stools could mean illness, malabsorption issues, or poor diet. These stools should be evaluated by a veterinarian but are not an emergency.

Blood in the Stool If you see blood in your Goldendoodle's stool, get her to the veterinarian immediately. Red blood indicates

Canine Cancer

Golden Retrievers have one of the highest cancer rates in the canine world and, sadly, Goldendoodles have become a part of that legacy. However, thanks to dramatic strides in genetic research and cancer research, promising progress is being made on many fronts in the battle against canine cancer. For the most up-to-date research, as well as ways you can participate and donate, see the links under "Cancer Research" on page 91.

a tear or injury somewhere in the colon. Dark blood indicates injury higher up in her system. Blood in the stool can also be a symptom of other serious health issues such as Parvo, colitis, or a parasitic or viral infection. The presence of blood and/or diarrhea requires an immediate trip to the veterinarian.

Diarrhea A puppy or dog with diarrhea is at risk for dehydration and should be taken to the veterinarian. There are any number of causes for diarrhea such as illness, bad food, or a parasitic infection. It is always best to get your dog to the veterinarian if diarrhea persists for more than one or two bowel movements in a day. And yes, the veterinarian will need a sample.

Constipation If your dog is straining to have a bowel movement and is unsuccessful, she may be constipated. If your Goldendoodle appears to be in pain, there may be a blockage in her intestinal tract and she should be taken to the veterinarian immediately. Symptoms of an intestinal blockage are discussed later in this chapter on pages 59–60.

Flatulence Although you may have laughed and gagged as a dog's flatulence has cleared a room, it isn't normal for a dog to be flatulent on a regular basis. If your dog's flatulence comes on suddenly and is accompanied by diarrhea, abdominal pain, or a loss of appetite, get her to the veterinarian right away.

Scooting and Chewing Contrary to popular belief, dogs who scoot their backsides on the floor or ground do not necessarily have worms. Scooting and chewing in the anal area can have several causes, including worms and anal gland impaction, all of which cause irritation to the anal area.

Infected or impacted anal glands are a source of irritation that is relieved by having the anal glands expressed. This is something you can do at home (if you have the stomach for it), or you can have your groomer or veterinary technician express the glands. Keep an eye out for any chewing activity and/or swelling at the base of your dog's tail, as this can indicate an anal gland infection, which requires veterinary care. Unless your Goldendoodle is recently shaved, this is something you have to check by feeling the area.

If you see worm segments or something resembling rice grains on your dog's back end or in her stool, it is likely the source of the scooting. Your Goldendoodle needs to get to the veterinarian for an accurate diagnosis and for proper medication.

Another cause for scooting could be that your dog has ingested something she is having difficulty passing through her anus. If your dog is a grass eater, blades of grass can get stuck there. Unpleasant as it may be, you can decrease your dog's distress by helping to remove the offending object.

Lastly, the lovely long, curly Goldendoodle fur can actually pose a problem in the rectal area. If fecal matter gets caught in the fur, it can create a foul smelling and uncomfortable mat. It can even prevent your dog from defecting, which is a painful and traumatic experience for both you and your dog. Have a pair of round-end safety scissors in your grooming bag, and very carefully trim/snip away at the mat. Or take her to your veterinarian or groomer for an immediate trim. Keep the anal area fur trimmed fairly short. If you take your Goldendoodle to a groomer, request a "sanitary trim."

The Front End

Dog Breath Your dog's breath should have a neutral odor or smell lightly of food if she has recently eaten. Puppy's breath has a slightly sweet odor. Bad breath is an indicator something is not right, and unless you know your dog recently ate something ghastly, chronic bad breath is cause for concern. Something as simple as plaque buildup on her teeth, which over time creates a host of health issues, can be solved by regular brushing. If the bad breath persists, see your veterinarian.

Vomiting vs. Regurgitation—Know the Difference It is not unusual for dogs to vomit, because they have a well-developed vomiting center in their brains. Vomiting is typically caused by eating hard-to-digest matter, such as grass, which irritates the stomach. However, like other bodily eliminations, vomiting can be indicative of bigger problems.

It helps your veterinarian make a diagnosis if you understand the difference between vomiting and regurgitation. Technically, regurgitation occurs when food in the esophagus is expelled, appearing unforced and without retching. In simple terms, your dog opens her mouth and the contents of the esophagus flow out. In contrast, vomiting is the forceful emptying of the stomach preceded by retching and often drooling. By noting your Goldendoodle's physical state when she empties her stomach, you can give your veterinarian significant clues as to the cause of her stomach upset.

Occasional vomiting is nothing to get too worried about; however, you want to inspect the vomitus to see what your dog is bringing back up. Clean up the vomitus immediately and completely. Dogs being dogs, they will go back and try to eat it. If it is undigested food, your puppy may be eating too fast, so try feeding smaller, more frequent meals.

If the vomitus looks like coffee grounds (old, partially digested blood), contains blood, or smells like feces, get your dog to the veterinarian immediately. It is possible your dog is suffering from a bowel obstruction, and she needs immediate medical attention.

Regurgitation is cause for concern because it can indicate a possible obstruction or narrowing of the esophagus. If accompanied by constant drooling, it means the dog cannot swallow her saliva. A complication of regurgitation is aspiration pneumonia caused by food aspirated into the lungs. If your dog is regurgitating, call your veterinarian immediately.

Projectile vomiting is a sign something is very wrong with your dog. The most common reason is a gastric outflow obstruction; however, there are diseases that cause projectile vomiting, so call your veterinarian immediately!

If your dog is vomiting up clear, frothy bile, the causes can range from gastritis to an obstruction or bloat. Again, call your veterinarian immediately. The exception to this can be young puppies. Young puppies sometimes throw up bile when their stomachs are empty, usually during the night or first thing in the morning after an extended period without a meal. Possible solutions are to feed her closer to bedtime, increase the number of meals she gets in a day, or give her a puppy cookie just before bed. If the problem persists (you guessed it!), call your veterinarian.

If your dog's efforts to vomit are unproductive, this is a symptom of GDV, better known as bloat. Once again, call your veterinarian immediately! Familiarize yourself with the symptoms of bowel obstructions and bloat; both are discussed later in this chapter on pages 60–61. Knowing the signs and symptoms may save your dog's life.

Motion sickness plagues many young dogs. The good news is your Goldendoodle will eventually outgrow it once her inner ears are fully developed. In the meantime, it is best to withhold food and water before traveling. Your veterinarian can prescribe a motion sickness medication for your dog to help ease her travel discomfort. If she continues to have regular motion sickness past the age of twelve months, consult your veterinarian.

The Underside

Urination If your dog appears to be having difficulty urinating, needs to "go" frequently, or is having accidents in the house after she is housetrained, she may have a urinary tract infection (UTI). Get her to the veterinarian as soon as possible.

PARASITES

Parasites are repulsive and disturbing . . . and they are actively searching for your dog. Your vigilance goes a long way to keeping your Goldendoodle parasite free.

Roundworm

Puppies are often infested with ascarids, otherwise known as roundworms. From birth until twelve weeks of age, puppies are treated every two weeks for roundworm. It is advisable to have a fecal sample analyzed to ensure there are no other worms, such as hookworm, whipworm, or tapeworm. If other worms are present, your veterinarian may prescribe a broad-spectrum dewormer. (Ongoing parasite treatment varies depending on where you live.) Work with your veterinarian to create a schedule of regular testing and treatment appropriate for your region of the country.

Heartworm

Heartworm is a mosquito-borne blood parasite that causes severe illness or even death. Again, work with your veterinarian to create a schedule of regular testing and treatment appropriate for your region. For example, in a northern climate with a prolonged hard freeze each winter, you may only need to treat for heartworm for half of the year (mosquitoes don't fly when it is below freezing!). People in warmer locations need to treat their dogs year round.

Ear Mites

How do you know if your dog has ear mites? Your dog will be scratching her ears, shaking her head repeatedly, or rubbing her head against anything and everything. If you see this behavior in your dog, take a peek in her ears. If you experience a strong, unpleasant odor and/or see a waxy, dark buildup, have your veterinarian analyze the gunk in your dog's ears and give you an appropriate treatment plan. Cleaning your dog's ears on a regular basis helps to keep ear mite infestation and infections at bay.

Fleas

Fleas spread very quickly, especially in the summer months. Worse, they can infest your home! A female flea produces about 2,000 eggs in her four-month life span. These eggs fall off your dog and can hide anywhere the dog spends time: in her bed and yours, on the furniture, in the carpet, and so on. You see flea dirt (fecal matter) before you see a flea, so check your dog's skin closely, especially on her belly. Fleas can be prevented with a monthly treatment or a flea collar. If your dog has fleas, consult your veterinarian to determine the best treatment and prevention. You will also need to rid your home of fleas.

How to Remove a Tick

Prevention is the best defense when it comes to ticks and tick-borne diseases. Check your dog immediately after she is in an area where she could pick up ticks. The best way to check for ticks is by running your hands and eyes all over your dog, paying particular attention to the head, lips, ears, neck, and feet. Some ticks are as small as a poppy seed! Be sure to check along the edges of your dog's lips and ears, including inside the small indentation on the lower edge of the ear flap. Check inside the ear as well; ticks will crawl into the ear canal. If the tick is in the ear canal, your veterinarian needs to remove it. Most dogs enjoy being checked for ticks because it feels like they are getting special attention and a bit of a massage!

If you find a tick, do not crush it. This can transmit disease. Drop the tick in a jar of rubbing alcohol to kill it. Dropping it in water or flushing it down the toilet does not kill the tick.

If you find an embedded tick, remove it as soon as possible. Before you begin, you need a few items:

- Rubber or latex gloves (or something to protect your hands from disease)
- Fine-tipped tweezers
- A small jar of rubbing alcohol
- Antiseptic
- Triple antibiotic ointment

Anatomically, the head is the weakest part of the tick, and you want to avoid it snapping off and remaining under the skin. Contrary to popular belief, applying oil or petroleum jelly to the tick does not cause it to back out of the skin. It does suffocate the tick and, in the process, causes it to regurgitate and deposit more disease-carrying saliva into your dog. Touching the tick with a match or lit cigarette has the same effect.

There are three methods you can employ to remove ticks:

1. With your hands protected, simply rub the tick in a fast, circular motion, maintaining your direction. After about a minute, the tick should back out of the skin.
2. Grab the tick with tweezers as close to the skin as possible right where the mouth and head enter the skin. Do not grasp the tick by the body, as you may break the exoskeleton and release the disease-carrying contents. Very gently, slowly, and steadily pull the tick. Be patient. Eventually, the tick will tire and loosen its grip.
3. Ask your veterinarian to recommend a tick-removal tool.

Once the tick has been removed, use an antiseptic to clean the wound left by the tick, and then apply a little triple antibiotic ointment. A scab will form and the wound site may be slightly inflamed due to the irritation caused by the tick's bite. Contact your veterinarian if the area is still inflamed after one week, as there may be an infection.

If your Goldendoodle has or had fleas, keep a close eye on her stools for any signs of tapeworms. Tapeworms are transmitted to dogs when they consume fleas during the course of normal grooming.

Ticks

Ticks are small, bloodsucking parasites. During your first visit to the veterinarian, talk about the types of ticks in your area, the diseases they carry, and the best way to prevent the effects and diseases resulting from a tick bite. Deer ticks carrying Lyme disease strike dogs and their owners in many parts of the country. Tick-borne diseases can be very serious, so tick prevention is critical. Often, a tick can transmit more than one pathogen, resulting in a polymicrobial infection; one bite may lead to multiple diseases—not the kind of bargain any dog owner wants. Products recommended by your veterinarian will kill the tick within 24 hours. It is critical the tick be removed or killed within thirty-six to forty-eight hours before it can release the disease-causing bacteria into the blood stream.

DISEASES

Parvovirus

The danger of parvovirus cannot be understated. It can kill your puppy. Your Goldendoodle is most vulnerable to a communicable disease such as parvovirus during her early months before her vaccinations are complete. You can help keep your Goldendoodle puppy healthy with these simple preventive steps.

- Keep your puppy in a carrier or on your lap while visiting the veterinarian and avoid letting her walk on the floor.
- Do not take her to pet supply stores until she is fully vaccinated.
- Begin training at home and enroll your puppy in a class once she is fully vaccinated.
- Before taking your Goldendoodle to a puppy class, talk to you veterinarian about the parvo risk in your area and if there have been any recent outbreaks.

- Keep your puppy away from areas where other dogs have relieved themselves.
- Socialization is critical for young puppies; however, make sure she only socializes with other dogs and puppies who are fully vaccinated and healthy.
- Have visitors to your home leave their shoes outside. You don't know where those shoes have been and what diseases they may be bringing into your home. Until your puppy has all of her vaccinations, you need to be very cautious.

Kennel Cough

Kennel cough is the broad term given to a group of highly contagious respiratory diseases. Most kennels and many obedience classes require dogs to be vaccinated for kennel cough before accepting them as boarders or class participants.

Influenza

Canine influenza is highly contagious. As with humans, different strains have different impacts. Symptoms are similar to those in people: sneezing, nasal discharge, and frequent coughing that lasts for a few days to a week. It is wise to talk to your veterinarian about which strains are in your area and the need for vaccination. If you plan to travel with your Goldendoodle, make sure she is vaccinated against canine flu.

Other Nasties

Dogs can acquire any number of nasty bacteria or protozoa in the course of their lives, and, unfortunately, you can't prevent all of them. However, with vigilance, you can

minimize the occurrences. Here are a few things to watch out for:

- Dogs can be disgusting in their choice of gastronomic delights. Make sure she isn't dining on canine delicacies such as dead animals or the fecal matter of other animals or birds. These harbor an array of dangerous bacteria and fungus.
- Don't let your Goldendoodle drink from puddles or streams. These are havens for giardia and leptospirosis, both of which can make your Goldendoodle very sick.

CARING FOR YOUR SICK GOLDENDOODLE

Taking Your Goldendoodle's Temperature

Your dog's temperature ranges from 100°F to 102.5°F (38°C to 39.5°C) with the average being 101.3°F (38.5°C). Canine temperature is taken rectally. Before you attempt to do this yourself, have your veterinarian show you the proper way to do it.

Until you get used to taking your dog's temperature, it is best to use two people—one to take the temperature, and the other to hold the dog in a steady position of either standing up or lying down. A digital thermometer works best and is the easiest to read. Read the manufacturer's instructions to learn how it operates.

Before you begin, clean the thermometer with rubbing alcohol and dry it off. Lubricate the end of the thermometer with a personal lubricant or petroleum jelly. Lift the tail and, with a gentle twisting motion, insert the end of the thermometer into the anal canal, and then follow the manufacturer's instructions.

Once you are finished, wash the thermometer thoroughly and disinfect it with alcohol. Make sure it is boldly labeled "FOR DOG USE ONLY!"

Giving Your Goldendoodle Medication

At some point in your dog's life, you will have to give her medication of some kind. Most canine medications come in chewable, beef-flavored tablets, and most dogs gobble them up like treats. But what if your dog is prescribed a drug that isn't made as a yummy beef chewable? Or what if your dog is fussy and turns her nose up at the chewable tablets?

The old-school method has you pry your dog's mouth open, pop in the offensive pill, clap the mouth shut, and stroke her throat until she swallows it . . . hopefully. Frankly, this should be a last resort to get medication into your dog.

If the medication is a chewable, beef-flavored type, the tablets can be cut in

quarters so they are roughly the same size as kibble. Another alternative is to grind the tablets into a rough powder with a mortar and pestle, and then mix it into her food with a spoonful of plain yogurt.

But what about the bitter-tasting pill? Your local pet supply store may carry a product designed to mask the bitter pill, such as a beef- or chicken-flavored wrap. These wraps are wonderful! Just put the pill into the wrap, close it up, and give it to your dog. She thinks she is getting a treat. But not all dogs are fooled.

Another alternative is hiding the offensive pill in a piece of cheese or meat. However, some dogs will sniff out the pill and refuse to eat it. Here is a way to get around your pill-sniffing dog. You need three cubes of cheese or meat to give one pill. Give your dog the first piece of plain cheese, which passes all inspections, and then quickly give her the cheese with the pill while (and this is key) keeping the third piece of plain cheese right in front of her nose. The middle piece of cheese with the pill in it becomes something she needs to consume to get to the next piece of cheese. This little trick works almost every time!

Remember, if you are using food to deliver medication, watch your dog's caloric intake, particularly for ongoing medication.

ALLERGIES

Allergies in dogs are generally caused by biting insects, such as fleas, and airborne and food allergens. Allergies frequently manifest in the skin and result in constant itching and scratching, which can lead to "hot spots" or open sores. It is important to work with your veterinarian to find the source of the allergic reaction.

Food Allergies

Food allergies can be detected by putting your dog on a diet of limited ingredients, free of any preservatives, colorings, or artificial flavorings. Work with your veterinarian to create a diet of ingredients your dog has never had. For example, switch to venison or kangaroo meat if your dog has always had chicken- and beef-based foods. There are a variety of hypoallergenic prescription diets available. When the symptoms are under control, various foods can be reintroduced, one at a time, to uncover what is causing your dog's allergy.

While they may not be the actual allergen, carbohydrates such as veggies, fruits, and grains can feed a yeast infection. If your dog is diagnosed with a yeast infection, restrict her carbohydrate intake.

Atopic Dermatitis

Your Goldendoodle is at an unfortunate disadvantage when it comes to allergens inhaled or absorbed through the skin. Both Golden Retrievers and Poodles have a genetic predisposition toward atopic dermatitis, also known as canine atopy. This is a lifelong allergy condition that begins to show itself between the ages of one and three.

It all begins when allergens such as fleas, pollen, dust mite droppings, house dust, mold, and any number of other irritants are inhaled or licked into the system. This provokes an immune response resulting in inflammation

and itchiness. Ears are often the first area affected, and your Goldendoodle may scratch and rub her ears. Watery eyes, sneezing, and a runny nose often accompany active licking of the legs and scratching of the underside. As the scratch and itch cycles continue, sores can develop and lead to bacterial and fungal infections. If your dog has these symptoms, ask your veterinarian to do a skin scrape and test for both bacterial and fungal infections in her skin.

If your Goldendoodle develops atopic dermatitis, it may be worthwhile to get a referral to a veterinary allergist.

INTESTINAL BLOCKAGES (BOWEL OBSTRUCTIONS)

The first thing to be said about intestinal blockages (bowel obstructions) is . . . *pick up your stuff!* Goldendoodles are mouthy dogs. They like to have things in their mouths. The number one cause of intestinal blockages is dogs and puppies ingesting things they find, often something smelly stolen from the laundry basket or left on the floor. They find things everywhere and are known to eat just about anything. Because a dog's esophagus is larger than her digestive track, there is a high probability an ingested foreign body will cause a blockage in either the stomach or the bowels. Swallowed tennis balls and toys are another common cause of bowel obstruction. While small tennis balls are cute, they are a choking and swallowing hazard for your mouthy Goldendoodle. Get a ball size recommendation from your veterinarian based on the size of your Goldendoodle.

Symptoms

The intestine can become partially or completely blocked. Vomiting and a lack of appetite may be some of the first symptoms you see. A partial blockage can cause, over the course of several weeks, sporadic vomiting and/or diarrhea. If the blockage is complete, your dog may experience continuous projectile vomiting. She may not pass any stool or gas.

What to Do

Get your Goldendoodle to the veterinarian immediately. An intestinal blockage can only be properly diagnosed with an X-ray. If a blockage is found, surgery is required to remove it and repair any damage that might have been done to the intestine.

The last thing to be said about intestinal blockages is . . . *pick up your stuff!*

BLOAT (GDV)

Gastric dilatation volvulus (GDV), commonly known as bloat, is a life-threatening emergency. The mortality rate for bloat is high. Survival hinges on early recognition and treatment.

Bloat can happen to any dog, but typically, it occurs in middle-aged and elderly dogs. Deep-chested, large-breed dogs, such as Standard Poodles and Golden Retrievers, have a predisposition to bloat, and it is something every Goldendoodle owner must be aware of and take precautions against. Ask your breeder if there are any hereditary tendencies toward GDV in either the sire or dam's lines. This knowledge allows you to take appropriate precautions. There is no screening test available for GDV.

The Anatomy of Bloat (GDV)

Bloat is a two-part event. The first part is the *gastric dilatation* where the stomach becomes distended with trapped food, fluid, and gas. As the contents of the stomach ferment, the volume of gas increases, as does the dog's distress. The pressure from the expanding stomach puts pressure on the other organs and the diaphragm, making it difficult for the dog to breathe. It can also compress the veins in the abdomen, preventing blood flow to the heart.

The second part is the *volvulus* (which may or may not accompany the gastric dilatation), when the stomach rotates on its axis. Once the stomach rotates, the contents are trapped, the building gas has no place to go, and the blood supply to the stomach is cut off. With no blood flow to the stomach, the stomach begins to die or *necrose*. Once the stomach rotates, the dog's condition deteriorates rapidly.

Symptoms

Typical symptoms of GDV are:

- A distended abdomen—when thumped with a finger, sounds like a tight, air-filled drum (in the early stages, the abdomen may not be distended but can feel somewhat tight)
- Pacing and restlessness; however, the dog may not look distressed
- Intense abdominal discomfort (possibly seen initially as a very "preoccupied" look on the dog's face)
- Whining or groaning when the abdomen is pressed
- A stiff-legged walk with the head hanging
- Unproductive retching or vomiting
- Excessive salivation; the saliva will be thick and rope-like
- Pale gums and tongue
- Rapid development of severe weakness and shock

Hereditary and General Risk Factors

The tricky thing about GDV is dogs without any of the usual risk factors can succumb to it. However, hereditary and general risk factors include:

- Large, deep-chested breeds; a category containing both Standard Poodles and Golden Retrievers
- An anxious temperament
- Increasing age (typically strikes dogs ages seven to twelve)
- Gender—male dogs are more likely to bloat than female dogs
- Genetics—a history of GDV in your dog's lineage (check with your breeder)

Dietary Risk Factors

- Feeding one meal per day
- Eating from raised bowls
- Strenuous exercise on a full stomach
- Gulping food
- Drinking large quantities of water just before or after a meal

Treatment

There is no home remedy for GDV. It is an acute medical emergency that requires immediate veterinary care. After a physical examination, an X-ray is taken to determine if there is a volvulus, a rotation of the stomach.

If your dog is in the first phase of GDV (gastric dilatation), the veterinarian may be able to relieve gas pressure by inserting a stomach tube. Next, the stomach is washed out and, with the support of intravenous fluids, food and fluids are withheld for thirty-six to forty-eight hours. After this period, food and water are slowly reintroduced. Your Goldendoodle may or may not require surgery, depending on the level of internal damage caused by the gastric dilatation.

If your Goldendoodle is experiencing a full GDV (gastric dilatation volvulus), your veterinarian will determine if there is a possibility of saving your dog through surgery or if it would be kinder to euthanize her.

Prevention

Nothing can prevent GDV. However, there are steps you can take to mitigate some of the risk factors.

- Look into prophylactic gastropexy—a laparoscopic surgical procedure in which the stomach is surgically stapled to the abdominal wall (gastropexy). Although this won't prevent the buildup of gas, it allows for an easier release of the gas. More important, it keeps the stomach from rotating. If there is a familial history of GDV, discuss the pros and cons of this procedure with your veterinarian. Not without its risks, this surgery is routinely performed on working military and police dogs to prevent bloat.

- Feed three to four small meals per day rather than one or two large meals.
- Keep your dog from gulping down her food by using a special bowl designed to slow down her consumption or use a feeding toy. There are quite a few toys on the market where you put your dog's kibble into the toy, and she must work to get the food. This dramatically slows her eating.
- Monitor how much water your dog consumes before and after eating. She needs to drink but keep her from consuming a large amount.
- Keep your dog quiet for at least an hour before eating and one to two hours after eating. This may require crating her or crating younger dogs who like to play with your at-risk dog right after a meal.

TOXIC FOODS AND SUBSTANCES

There are human foods that are very toxic to dogs. Chief among them are xylitol, onions, chocolate, grapes, and raisins. It is critical you make any children in your home and neighborhood aware of this. Here is a partial list of some of the more common toxic foods; your veterinarian can provide you with a complete list or check the ASPCA website (*www.aspca.org*) or smartphone app. Keep in mind, the toxic effects of some of these foods are not immediate.

- Chocolate—toxins: theobromine and caffeine. Both are cardiac stimulants and diuretics.
- Grapes and raisins—toxin: unknown. Grapes and raisins can be toxic when consumed in large quantities (9 ounces (252 g) or more) and can result in kidney failure.
- Xylitol—a common, naturally derived sugar substitute, causes hypoglycemia (low blood sugar) in dogs. It also causes acute and life-threatening liver disease. A very small amount is needed to produce toxic effects in your dog. Depending on the size of your dog, a single piece of chewing gum can be deadly. After ingesting xylitol, dogs can begin to vomit and develop hypogly-

Check Your Peanut Butter!

Peanut butter manufacturers sometimes add xylitol as a sweetener. Xylitol is a natural sweetener derived from hardwoods, birch bark, corn cobs, and other sources. Because xylitol is a natural sweetener, do not think an "all natural" peanut butter cannot contain this canine toxin.

Check the ingredients each and every time you buy peanut butter, even if it is the same brand you've been buying, to make sure the manufacturer has not changed the ingredients to include xylitol. Xylitol can sicken and kill your dog within hours of ingestion.

cemia within thirty to sixty minutes. Some dogs develop liver failure within twelve to twenty-four hours after ingestion.

- The seeds, stems, or leaves of apples, plums, apricots, cherries, and peaches—toxin: cyanogenic glycosides. Cyanide poisoning can result.
- Onions or onion powder—toxin: thiosulfate. This toxin causes hemolytic anemia, which is a breakdown of red blood cells, leaving your dog short of oxygen.
- Coffee grounds and beans, tea leaves—toxin: caffeine, which is a cardiac stimulant and diuretic.
- Wild mushrooms—toxins vary depending on the mushroom. If you discover your Goldendoodle eating any mushroom you didn't buy at the market, watch her closely. If any symptoms of illness appear, get her to the veterinarian immediately.
- Spinach—although not toxic to dogs in general, it can have detrimental effects on dogs with kidney problems. Spinach is high in oxalic acid, which removes calcium from the blood. Kidney damage can be expected as the calcium is removed from the blood in the form of calcium oxalate, which then obstructs the kidney tubules.
- Macadamia nuts—toxin: unknown. A small quantity (as few as six) can cause accelerated heart rate, tremors in the skeletal muscles, elevated body temperature, and weakness or paralysis of the hindquarters.
- Tobacco—toxin: nicotine, which affects the nervous and digestive systems.
- Yeast dough—the dough expands to many times its original size when it reaches

Toxic Plants

Many plants common to our gardens and homes (including the dead leaves) are poisonous to your Goldendoodle. To be sure your home and yard are safe, check the ASPCA website for a long list of toxic plants at *www.aspca.org*. Or, like so many things today, there's an app for your smartphone: Animal Poison by ASPCA—dogs, cats, birds, and horses.

your Goldendoodle's warm stomach. This expansion, and the gas produced, is very dangerous for your dog. Since the Goldendoodle is, by virtue of her parentage, at risk for GDV (bloat), this large amount of rapidly accumulating gas can

be deadly. The alcohol released from the fermenting yeast is also toxic.

- Alcohol—your dog is much smaller than you and has a much lower tolerance for alcohol; therefore, she is much more vulnerable to its toxic effects.

Antifreeze

Antifreeze has a sweet taste dogs (and cats) like, and a very small amount is enough to kill your Goldendoodle. Clean up any spills immediately and thoroughly. If you think your Goldendoodle has ingested antifreeze, get her to your veterinarian or emergency clinic immediately. There is an antifreeze antidote available, but it must be administered soon after ingestion. There are animal-friendly brands of antifreeze available.

SEASONAL CHANGES

When the seasons change, you need to be tuned into your dog. Watch her behavior and look for signs that she is uncomfortable. This becomes even more critical as your dog gets older or if she's under a year old.

Hypothermia and Frostbite

Once the temperature drops below freezing, keep a close eye on your Goldendoodle. The colder it gets, the shorter the time she can be outside. Once the temperature goes below zero, she goes out, does her business, and comes back in the house immediately. She should *never* be left unattended outdoors in cold weather. If you are not going outside with her, keep an eye on her from the door or a window.

Winter Gear

Depending on the size of your Goldendoodle, children's pajamas and dog boots do a terrific job of keeping the snow out of the fur—just be sure to cut holes in the appropriate elimination areas.

Let your Goldendoodle's coat grow out during the winter months. Her coat keeps her warm, so keep it in good shape. Keep her nails, foot fur, and the fur between her pads trimmed to minimize the formation of painful snowballs between the pads.

When she goes outside to play or for walks, keep an eye on her feet, especially if your neighbors use salt and ice melt. Keep a damp washcloth near the door and wipe her feet off as soon as you get home. Salt causes sores on the pads and, depending on the type used, ice melt can be dangerous if ingested when she licks her paws. There are many great footwear options for dogs at both your local pet supply store and online.

If you have a very young or aging dog, or it is very cold outside, get her an insulated dog coat, preferably one that blocks the wind. If your Goldendoodle has longer hair, putting a sweater on her keeps the snow from gathering in her fur.

What about the snowballs that form on your Goldendoodle's legs in the winter? Break up the snowballs with your fingers as best as you can, or use a very warm washcloth to wrap around the snowballs to melt them. Then keep her warm while she drip-dries.

Toweling her while there is still snow in her fur creates mats, so gently pat her dry as the snow melts. This is a good time to wrap your Goldendoodle in a blanket and snuggle. When your dog's fur is wet, it loses its ability to retain heat and keep her warm.

So, what are the signs your dog is too cold? The most noticeable one is lifting her foot and holding it up off the ground. Check her ears and feet with your bare hand—if they're cold, your dog is cold. Your dog may also start to shiver, a warning sign of possible hypothermia.

Watch for signs of frostbite. In dogs, frost-bitten skin appears red, purple, or gray. If it

looks like your dog is suffering from frost-bite, wrap her feet (or the affected part) in a blanket or towel (you can warm them in your dryer—just don't make them hot), and gradually warm her up. Check her ears, particularly the ends of her ear flaps. If they are cold or the skin appears frostbitten, hold the ear flaps between your hands to warm them. Contact your veterinarian immediately.

Signs of hypothermia include violent shivering, nonresponsiveness, disorientation, and stumbling. Most cases of hypothermia are the result of the dog falling through ice. If you are near a frozen lake, pond, or river, keep a very close watch on your Goldendoodle!

If your dog is showing signs of hypothermia, take her temperature. A dog's normal body temperature is 101.5°F (39°C). If your dog's temperature is below 100°F (38°C), call your veterinarian immediately.

If your Goldendoodle is suffering from hypothermia, you need to warm her, but not too quickly. Lying down with your dog and wrapping the two of you in a blanket is a good way to slowly warm up your dog.

Protect Your Goldendoodle from Heatstroke

Never, ever leave your Goldendoodle in the car on a warm day. Although the air outside the car may feel pleasant and cool to you, it doesn't take very long for the interior of a car, whether it is in the shade or direct sunlight, to heat up to dangerous levels for your dog.

In hot, humid weather, limit your Goldendoodle's exercise. Choose the cooler parts of the day for walks and, even if she gives you the biggest, saddest eyes, do not take her running.

Make sure your Goldendoodle has access to shade, grass, and fresh, cool water. If you must leave your Goldendoodle in the yard while you are away, make sure the shade is continuous and doesn't disappear as the sun moves across the sky.

Heatstroke (Hyperthermia)

Unlike humans, dogs cannot sweat to cool themselves. A dog's primary method of cooling is panting and, to a very negligible degree, sweating through her foot pads. Because of their limited ability to cool themselves, dogs cannot tolerate high temperatures. While you may be comfortable in warm to hot weather, your Goldendoodle is not. Watch her carefully.

Signs of Heatstroke

- The first indication your dog is overheated is heavy panting and labored breathing.
- Your dog may begin salivating heavily. The saliva will be thick and rope-like.
- Your dog may vomit.
- Mucous membranes and the tongue may appear bright red or grayish and pale.
- Your dog may appear to be disorientated or confused.
- Your Goldendoodle may have difficulty walking or even standing.
- Her rectal temperature is above 104°F (40°C).

What to Do

- First, move your dog into an air-conditioned building if possible.
- Call your veterinarian and make arrangements to transport your dog to his/her office.
- Take her temperature every few minutes to determine when it returns to normal range. Do not overcool her—that creates a whole different set of problems.
- Begin to try to cool your dog. Use cool, not cold, water on her legs and trunk. Cold water or ice causes the capillaries at the surface of the skin to contract and inhibit the flow of cooled blood.
- Use a fan to speed the evaporation and cooling process. This gently cools the blood in the capillaries near the surface of the skin where the circulatory system then transfers the cooled blood to the core.
- Apply rubbing alcohol to her paw pads to help the cooling.
- Do not force your Goldendoodle to drink water.
- Heatstroke can bring on serious complications. Make sure your dog is not alone for any length of time until you can get her to the veterinarian.

Training

There is more to training than obedience commands. How you interact with your Goldendoodle from the beginning sets the stage for her future behavior.

From the day you bring her home, treat your Goldendoodle puppy like she's a full-grown dog. Don't encourage any behavior you don't want in a full-grown dog.

A second pearl of wisdom is to be consistent. It won't be easy; however, consistency pays huge dividends. If you tell your puppy to sit, make sure she sits. Do not let her ignore you. You must gently, but firmly, follow through on all commands even if it doesn't seem to matter anymore. Don't think, "I'll get her the next time," because by doing this, your puppy learns listening to you is optional. It makes training your puppy more difficult and may put her in danger. The time will come when it's critical that she obey your commands.

BEHAVIOR-BASED TRAINING

When your Goldendoodle puppy comes home, she doesn't know right from wrong. The only way she learns it is through experience and training. If your puppy does something and receives a positive result, such as a treat or a pat on the head, she will repeat the behavior. If she does something and gets a negative result, such as being ignored or a verbal correction, she will not repeat the behavior. Now, it takes a few times for her to realize this, but with consistency, she will get the message. Consistency is the key to effective training. It is important everyone in the home, including guests, understand and follow the rules set out for the puppy.

Positive Behavior

Reinforce when your puppy does something positive. For example, if your puppy

A Training Resource

Barron's Dog Training Bible by Andrea Arden is an exceptional training resource for both new and experienced dog owners. It is an in-depth look at canine behavior, obedience training, how to socialize your dog in a positive and safe manner, remedying behavioral issues, fun activities to do with your dog, tricks training, and more.

barks to go outside, gently greets a visitor, or politely sits while you eat dinner, praise her. Use phrases such as *"Good puppy," "That's right,"* or *"Yes."* Make certain the praise is given immediately after the positive behavior so she makes the association. This is called reward-based training and it is an effective, fun, and compassionate way for your Goldendoodle to learn good behavior.

Negative Behavior

Negative actions such as digging through the trash, dragging a roll of toilet paper through the house, or raiding the clothes hamper are actually fun for your pup. Consequently, she will continue these actions until you teach her otherwise.

Change of Focus Remove the stimulus for the negative behavior, put her in a *sit*, wait four seconds, and then calmly reward her for the *sit* with a ball or a favorite toy to redirect her behavior.

Verbal Corrections Select a word or sound to use when your puppy does something wrong, such as *"No,"* *"Enough,"* or *"Eh-eh."* Use a low voice (a high voice is a reward), and be short, firm, and nonemotional—just enough to get her attention. Then physically remove her from the situation. Your puppy will soon associate the correction with ceasing her current activity.

Ignore Her Ignoring your puppy is a challenge, especially when she is barking for attention, food, playtime, and so on. To ignore her, turn away, look at the ceiling, or leave the room. She eventually learns barking doesn't get her the desired attention.

Time-out If your puppy behaves badly, give her a time-out. This can be done by tethering her to a chair with a short leash or confining her to a small room, or anywhere there is nothing to play with or chew. Keep her confined for thirty seconds and then let her free, but only if she is not barking. If you leave her in time-out for over thirty seconds, she forgets why she is there. Repeat time-out until she understands.

Note: Never put your Goldendoodle in her crate when you are upset or angry. The crate is not a tool for punishment. If you must crate her make sure your tone is happy. Do not force her into the crate. Only good things should happen in the crate.

Training is a fun, cooperative experience for you and your puppy. If you put energy and enthusiasm into behavior-based training, you will have a well-mannered puppy in no time. Just remember, consistency is the key to training success.

CRATE TRAINING

A crate is one of the best things for your Goldendoodle puppy, because it serves as a private den where she can retreat safely and securely. Here are a few positive benefits of crate training:

- It provides a safe place to be away from others.
- It offers a place for good, solid rest.
- It facilitates housetraining—dogs don't soil the space where they sleep.
- It makes for a comfortable bed and sleeping environment.
- It serves as a temporary playpen when you are unable to monitor her.

Crate training promotes positive discipline and routine for your puppy. Teach your Goldendoodle (no matter what age) that the crate is the best place in the world. Every interaction your dog has with her crate must be pleasant.

How to Crate Train

Never place the crate in an out-of-the-way place. Make your puppy's crate part of the family environment. A good location for the crate is a central room in the home, such as the living room or kitchen. Consider having more than one crate. Why? Place one in the busiest part of the house for daytime use and place another in the bedroom for nighttime use. Make sure the crate is in a temperature-controlled environment, away from drafts, so your puppy isn't too hot or too cold. Wherever you crate her, give your new puppy a few days to get used to her new den, and praise her every time she goes near it.

Guide your Goldendoodle to her crate, door closed, with some treats or a toy tucked inside. The goal is to get your puppy so interested in getting inside that she paws and begs you to open the door. Now open the door, let her enter the crate, and praise her with words such as "*Good dog*" or "*Yes*" and lots of pats. The first few times, leave the door open, and when she comes out, ignore her. Downplay the exit so she doesn't interpret outside of the crate being better than inside. If she doesn't enter the crate right away, do not try to force her. At this early stage use only inductive methods.

Once she is going in on her own, begin closing the door for a few seconds. Repeat this exercise several times, each time increasing the amount of time she is in the crate with the door shut. Your puppy may start whining, barking, or scratching the door. If this is the case, tell her to "*Sit*," and then wait five seconds before opening the door so she doesn't associate whining, barking, or scratching with being released from the crate. Make her next confinement shorter and start building up the time again. You want this to be a positive

experience. When your puppy has this routine down, start adding the word "*Crate*" or "*Kennel*" as she enters the crate. Soon, your puppy knows to go to the crate no matter where you are in the house.

For crating overnight, you may need to place your puppy in her crate and shut the door upon retiring. If the crate is next to your bed, you can easily reach over and offer a reassuring word or a quick pet through the wire. Give her a sturdy chew in her crate at bedtime to act as a pacifier. Make sure she is warm enough; remember, she is used to sleeping in a pile of warm puppies.

After introducing your Goldendoodle to the crate, begin feeding regular meals there. If your puppy readily enters, put the food dish in the back of the crate. If she is still reluctant to go inside, put the dish only as far inside as she will voluntarily go without becoming fearful or anxious. Each time you feed her, position the dish a little farther back in the crate. Once your puppy is standing comfortably in the crate to eat her meal, you can close the door. When you begin this training,

Do Not Use the Crate When

- the puppy has diarrhea;
- the puppy is vomiting;
- the puppy has not eliminated shortly before being placed inside the crate;
- the puppy has not had sufficient exercise, companionship, and socialization.

open the door as soon as she finishes her meal. With each subsequent feeding, leave the door closed a few minutes longer until she stays in the crate for ten to fifteen minutes after eating. However, if there is a history of bloat in your puppy's lineage, it is critical to keep her quiet for an hour or two after meals—the crate is the perfect place for her to take a post-meal nap.

Spend the next couple of days practicing these exercises, and while your puppy is in the crate, practice going in and out of the room, checking in every few minutes to get her accustomed to seeing you coming and going.

When you let her out of the crate, quietly and calmly open the door and direct her outside to the designated potty area. (If it is morning, you may need to pick her up because your puppy will never make it outdoors before she eliminates.) Repeat this process a few times before you leave for longer periods. Always make sure your puppy empties her bladder before you go. Start slowly and build up to longer periods of time away from your puppy. Consider leaving on music, as this creates a comfortable and familiar atmosphere for your puppy.

Do not leave food or water inside the crate while the puppy is unattended. However, if your puppy is to be confined for more than two hours, add a small hamster-type water dispenser for her.

Cautions About the Crate

The crate serves as a safe place for your puppy; however, there are some rules to keep in mind.

- The crate should never be used for punishment. Brief, happy time-outs are okay.
- Do not overuse the crate. This is not where your Goldendoodle lives. Limit crate time to no more than eight hours total in a twenty-four-hour period.
- Never force your Goldendoodle into her crate. Tossing in a favorite treat is a much easier way to get her in the crate.

Separation Anxiety

If your puppy has separation anxiety, confinement may escalate the problem. Behaviors resulting from separation anxiety include:

- continuous barking for thirty minutes or longer
- urination or defecation in the crate
- damage to the crate
- moving of the crate
- wet chest fur from drooling and salivation on the floor
- consistently destructive behavior when the puppy is left alone
- following you from room to room
- frantic greetings upon your return

If your puppy has excessive separation anxiety problems, talk to your veterinarian or a professional trainer about solutions.

Important Tips Regarding the Crate

- Always remove your puppy's collar before she enters the crate. If you must keep the collar on for identification purposes, use a safety "breakaway" collar.
- If your puppy messes in the crate while you are out, do not punish her. Simply wash out the crate with a pet odor neutralizer. The goal is to have no accidents. If one occurs, review and reevaluate your schedule, the puppy's eating and drinking schedule, and, most critical, how often she is allowed to relieve herself. It is up to you to set her up for success.
- Do not allow children to play in your Goldendoodle's crate or to handle her while she is in the crate. The crate is her private getaway. Respect her space.

HOUSETRAINING

Vigilance best describes the state of mind required when housetraining a puppy. Puppies need to eliminate after playing, eating, drinking, waking up . . . and anytime in between.

Cleanup on Aisle 5!

OOPS! Accidents happen! It is part of owning a puppy.

As a new Goldendoodle owner, you quickly learn that your first priority is housetraining. Patience and vigilance are required during this process. Every puppy is different and it can take a few weeks for a puppy to be fully housetrained.

From the first day, train her to eliminate outside of the house. Dogs naturally develop preferences for going in certain places or on distinct surfaces, such as grass or mulch. If you don't proactively train her to go outside, she will choose a place inside your home. The keys to housetraining are consistency and reward.

It is important to know how often your puppy eliminates. If she eats, drinks, or plays excessively, she needs to go more often. Give your puppy plenty of opportunities—she can't hold it for long periods of time. Closely supervise her any time she is not confined to her crate or confinement area. If she begins to circle or squat, scoop her up and take her outside to the designated elimination area.

How Long Can My Puppy Hold It?

How long puppies can comfortably hold their bladders depends on their size and their age. Generally speaking, at two months a puppy can hold it for two hours. At four months, four hours; six months, six hours; and at seven months, most puppies are able to hold their bladders for eight hours. Now, if your four-month-old puppy can't go more than two hours without an accident, then work within her schedule and provide timely potty breaks. (If your puppy is urinating with a great deal of frequency, this may indicate a urinary tract infection. Contact your veterinarian.)

Consistency Is Key

Develop a sleeping, eating, playing, and napping routine to establish patterns for her. For example, your pup goes outside when she first wakes up and before she retires to her crate for the night. She should also go out

Goldendoodle is easily distracted. Keep her on a leash and take her directly to the designated elimination area every time.

Praise and Reward Work Like Magic

When your Goldendoodle eliminates, praise her in your regular tone of voice so you don't startle her. Simply praise and treat her the instant she is done eliminating. Timing is critical. If you delay the praise and treat, you are rewarding her for walking to the house, not eliminating outside.

Prevent Accidents

Supervise You can supervise your puppy by keeping her on a leash, using gates, closing doors, and so on. Be alert. If your puppy suddenly runs out of the room, she may be looking for a secret spot to eliminate. Every time your puppy eliminates in your house it reinforces a habit—a bad habit. The puppy must be supervised at all times. If you cannot supervise her, put her in her crate with a sturdy chew toy.

Caught in the Act If your puppy is caught in the act, say (no yelling!), "*Outside*" (once

within thirty minutes of eating, so scheduling meals at the same time every day helps you know when to let her out.

When you are about to take your puppy outside, use a trigger word, such as "*Outside*," "*Potty*," or "*Business*." Say this word *every time* you take her out to help her make the association. Say it with enthusiasm and a happy expression on your face—even if it's at 5:00 A.M.!

When you take her outside, stay with her until she has done her business. Not all puppies completely empty their bowels or bladder on the first go; she may need a second or third elimination.

When puppies go outside, they want to do everything *but* their business. With so many smells and interesting things to explore, your

Cleaning Up Accidents

If you find a puddle or pile, simply clean it up. Use a pet-odor neutralizing cleanser or, if not available, use white distilled vinegar, soap, and water. Do not use ammonia-based cleansers because they smell like urine to your dog.

is enough) and whisk her off to her elimination spot outside. In your normal, neutral voice, say, "*Potty.*" Then ask yourself what *you* missed, not the puppy; she has no blame here. You either did not follow the schedule or missed her cues.

After-the-Fact Discipline Does Not Work! Never correct (verbally or otherwise) your puppy or dog for house-soiling accidents you did not witness. Never. She will have no idea why you are angry and this will only serve to confuse her. You are more to blame than she is.

Never Discipline Submissive Urination When a puppy is overly excited, or feeling submissive, she can urinate involuntarily. Typical triggers of submissive urination are eye contact, verbal scolding, hovering over, reaching out to pet your puppy's head, animated movements, and talking in an excited or loud voice, as well as strangers/visitors approaching your puppy. Don't punish your puppy for this behavior or the problem could get worse. Don't worry; she will eventually grow out of it.

Housetraining Problems

If you have a difficult time housetraining your puppy, ask yourself the following questions:

✔ Did I leave her alone too long? If "yes," take her outside more frequently.
✔ Was I too focused on my phone/computer/ game and missed her cues? Set alarms on your devices to remind you to take the puppy outside.
✔ Is the crate or room too big? If "yes," block off part of the extra space.

Intelligent Pup

Goldendoodles can be a bit too smart. They can, and will, discern patterns. If your training pattern consists of *sit, down, rollover,* don't be surprised when your Goldendoodle demonstrates the entire sequence when you tell her to *sit.* Once you finish laughing, try to think of ways you can change up the routine.

✔ Is she drinking too much water out of boredom or habit? If "yes," consider giving her less water and involve her in activities to break the boredom.
✔ Could she have a urinary tract problem or other medical condition? If "yes" or "maybe," talk to your veterinarian.

Housetraining Signals

Using a bell or teaching her to speak are two very effective methods to help your Goldendoodle let you know when she needs to go outside.

Bell Method At the door where you take your puppy in and out for elimination, hang a small bell at the height of your puppy's nose. Each time you take her outside, physically take her nose or paw, ring the bell, then open the door. Your puppy will soon correlate the two and run to the door to ring the bell herself.

Speak on Command Teach her to speak when she needs to eliminate. When you are at the door, say, "*Outside? Speak!*" When she gives one bark, praise her, open the door, and take her outside. This is a great command because it can be used anywhere, at any door. ("Basic Commands: Speak" on page 78.)

BASIC COMMANDS

Begin training at home. Start with short sessions, and always end on a positive note. If she can't master a particular command, end the session with one she has mastered.

There are several different training methodologies: capturing, shaping, targeting, and luring. Because it often works best with puppies, luring is the method taught below. Luring involves calling attention to your hand, which is holding a reward, such as a small treat or a toy.

Sit

Stand or squat in front of your puppy and hold the treat (the lure) right above her nose. Move your hand up and back toward her tail. She will naturally lower her rear end to the ground. When her bottom is firmly planted on the floor (you want a solid *sit*, not a squat), mark the behavior with a click or a "*Yes*," and give her the reward. Once she begins sitting when she sees the hand movement, begin adding the command "*Sit*" when her bottom is correctly placed on the floor.

Down

Lure your puppy into a *sit*, and then hold the treat in front of her nose. In a downward sweeping motion, slowly lower your hand, palm down, moving your hand toward her chest, and then to the floor between her front paws. Keep your hand between her front legs and on the floor. When her belly touches the floor, mark the behavior with a click or

a "*Yes*," and give her the reward. Once she begins to drop into the down position when she sees the sweeping motion of your hand, begin adding the command "*Down*" when her belly touches the floor.

Leave It

You will need two types of treats for this exercise. Place a low-value treat, such as a piece of her daily kibble, on the floor. As she moves toward the low-value treat, cover it with your hand. When she stops, mark the pause by rewarding her with a high-value treat (one of her favorites) from your other hand. Never give her the low-value *leave it* treat. You want to teach her that "*Leave it*" means to leave it forever.

Work up to a five second pause before marking and rewarding. When she consistently waits five seconds, begin to introduce the "*Leave it*" command right before giving her the reward.

Out/Give/Drop

The "*Out/Give/Drop*" command has many uses, from ending a game of tug, getting your dog to release the ball when playing fetch, dropping a dead animal she picked up, or, and this is the very best one, making her release the live animal she has just caught.

Out/Give/Drop is similar to *leave it*, in that you are exchanging one thing for another. Begin with giving her a favorite toy or a ball. Have a high-value treat in your hand and hold it in front of her nose. When she drops the toy, mark the behavior with a click or a "*Yes*," and give her the reward. As you are giving her the reward, reach down and grab the toy with your other hand; she doesn't get to have the treat and take back the toy. Once she is reliably dropping the toy or ball, choose your preferred command for this, and begin to introduce the "*Out/Give/Drop*" command right before giving her the reward.

Stay

Once your puppy can *sit* on command, stand directly in front of her, holding your palm in front of her face. Keeping your palm at your puppy's eye level, take two steps back and count to three. If she stays in her spot, mark it with a click or a "*Yes*," step back to her, and reward her. If she tries to follow you, say "*Eh,eh*" in a low voice and begin again. With each success, gradually increase the time between giving her the hand signal and when you mark and reward her, all the while giving her quiet, verbal praise.

When she is reliable using the hand signal, introduce the command "*Stay*" and begin to increase your distance.

Come

Teaching your Goldendoodle to come when called is the most critical of all the commands—it could, quite literally, save her life someday. Practice this command at every opportunity, every day.

You do not want to use the "*Come*" command unless you are 99.99 percent sure your puppy will come to you. You can make a kiss noise or clap your hands to encourage her to come to you. Once she is reliable with the noises, you can add the "*Come*" command.

If you've been using the "*Come*" command and she isn't responding, you may have poi-

soned the command. Don't worry—you can start training again, just with another word, such as "*Here*."

When you begin training at home, you can use some of her kibble or small training treats as rewards; just be sure you subtract it from her daily food allotment—you don't want to overfeed her. When you begin training in places with more distractions, bring out the high-value treat, such as freeze-dried liver or dried beef lung, and reserve these just for recall work.

The Ping-Pong game is a great way to begin recall training for your Goldendoodle puppy. Enlist the help of a friend or a family member, then sit on the floor about 5–6 feet (1.5–2 m) apart in a room with minimal distractions. While Person A gently restrains the puppy,

Training Name

Because a dog's name can be overused, be sure she has a "training name." Reread "What's in a Name?" on page 30.

Person B makes kiss noises or claps softly to get the puppy's attention, then extends a hand out, showing the treat to the puppy as Person A releases the puppy. As the puppy moves toward Person B, Person B marks the approach with "*Yes*," "*Good girl*," and other words of encouragement. When the puppy arrives at Person B, the puppy gets the treat and is praised wildly. Then the action is reversed and the puppy goes back to Person A. This can also be done using a tug toy and a game of tug as the reward.

After a dozen or so successful repetitions, you can begin to insert the word you have decided to use for the recall, such as "*Come*," "*Here*," and so on.

Once she is reliable inside the house, it is time to graduate to the great outdoors; however, make sure it is the securely fenced great outdoors. This is where you want not only high-value treats, but also a 20- to 30-foot (6- to 9-m) long line attached to your Goldendoodle's collar. When you are feeling confident in her recall outdoors, keep the long line attached to her collar, and drop the long line. Just be prepared to step on it if she gets distracted and starts to run off. Adding a knot every few feet in the long line will keep it from slipping under your shoe.

Not Coming When Called The number one rule when your dog does not *come* when called is *do not chase her*! This may sound counterintuitive, but the best thing to do is wave your arms (dogs cue off of movement) to get her attention and call her in a happy, excited voice. Then turn around and *walk or run away from your Goldendoodle*. When she comes, enthusiastically praise her as you clip on her leash or long line.

Practice this in controlled environments, such as a fenced yard, a canine training facility with an indoor arena, or a fenced outdoor arena you can rent. Dogs are pack animals, and their instinct is to follow the pack leader.

Speak

The "*Speak*" command is useful, particularly when housetraining your dog. Find your puppy's favorite toy and shake it in front of her until she is so excited she lets out a bark. The moment she barks, mark it, and either treat her or give her the toy. Repeat this exercise, and once she is consistently barking just one time for the toy, begin to add the command "*Speak*."

COUNTER SURFING

The best way to prevent your Goldendoodle from stealing food from the counter is to not leave food on the counter. However, this is not how most people live, and it is best to train your Goldendoodle to stay off the counters, if for no other reason than that some human foods can be fatal to dogs.

To begin, use a gate to restrict your dog's access to the kitchen. For the purposes of training, you want her to have access only when you are in the kitchen. Depending on her speed and temperament, you may want to have a leash on her. Now place something yummy on the counter. When she looks in the direction of the item, tell her "*Leave it!*" in a low, calm voice. If she looks away, give her a treat (something even yummier than what is on the counter) and lots of praise.

It would be wonderful if this was all it took, but if you have a very food-motivated

Goldendoodle, you need to employ more creative methods. Your dog is going to behave differently when you are not in the room, so if you are not there to tell her *Leave it!* she may still consider the chicken left to cool on the counter as fair game. After all, you left it within her reach, didn't you? Also, if she consumes that chicken and its cooked bones, it could cause an emergency trip to the veterinarian. Chicken bones (or any cooked bones) are dangerous because they can splinter and damage your Goldendoodle's stomach and intestines.

If the first method doesn't work, you can try setting a booby trap for her. Take a cookie sheet and put a fistful or two of coins on it. Again, put something yummy on the counter, but this time place the cookie sheet in front of it, with it balanced on the edge of the counter. When she jumps up to steal the food, she will tip over the cookie sheet and be startled (but not harmed) by the sudden noise and activity. This can often cure a counter surfer on the first try.

You can also purchase counter pads (search for "pet electronic training mat" online), which deliver a small electrical shock to the dog when her paw(s) touch the pad. Giving shocks or zaps to a dog is rarely a recommended deterrent, but if you have a real problem with your Goldendoodle counter surfing, you may want to look into one of these products. Or, preferably, put a permanent gate across the entrance to your kitchen.

SOCIALIZATION

Your new puppy needs two kinds of socialization: with people and with other puppies

Doodle Play Groups

Getting together with other doodle owners in your area is a great way for you and your Goldendoodle to socialize. Check social media for local doodle groups or ask your veterinarian for recommendations. Try to find a Doodle play group that meets at different owners' homes. These groups are usually comprised of good owners who watch their dogs. The dogs should have similar play behaviors and be approximately the same size. Minis may need to play separately.

and dogs. The quality of these interactions is more important than the quantity. One poor experience can undo weeks of positive work. Remember, your puppy must be fully vaccinated and cleared by your veterinarian for these activities!

Meeting People

If your puppy can have 100 positive interactions with people in her first month with you, she will be well on her way to becoming well socialized. The key is for these interactions to all be positive and, most important, varied. She needs to meet people of all races, ages, sizes, and genders wearing a variety of outerwear, such as hats, uniforms, coats, and even facial hair. She also needs to become acquainted with the things people carry or use, such as walkers, strollers, briefcases, backpacks, umbrellas, and so on.

You must control her social interactions to ensure her experiences are positive. Most people, particularly children, have no idea that their squeals of delight or rapid approach may actually scare a puppy. Ask friends or family members who the puppy does not know if they would be willing to help you teach your puppy that people are wonderful; someone will be willing to help you.

Ask your helper to stand, or kneel, and stay still and calm. Slip the leash under your foot, so if your puppy tries to jump you can stop her. Give your helper a treat for the puppy, then allow the puppy to choose whether or not she wants to approach the person. If she does approach, have your helper offer the treat and quietly say hello. If your puppy chooses not to approach the person, it means she does not feel safe. Do not force a greeting. Respect her feelings, thank the person for helping you, and then turn and walk away. If your puppy is hesitant with strangers, more work is needed with people she knows before trying strangers again.

Meeting Dogs

Play with other puppies is a very important part of your Goldendoodle's development. Most good training programs provide time in each session for this type of interaction. You want your puppy to have regular interactions with dogs of different ages and sizes, preferably off leash, as body language is not inhibited and your Goldendoodle can make the choice whether or not to interact.

Because every dog has a play style, finding a play group moderated by a trainer helps to ensure dogs are properly matched to dogs with similar play styles.

Dog Parks—Be Cautious

Dog parks are not well regulated. Most people who bring their dogs to dog parks are not experts in dog behavior, and they may insist that their dogs are just playing when they are actually exhibiting potentially aggressive behavior, which may cause a dog fight. Others think their dogs' aggressive

behavior is just "alpha" behavior, when the dogs are actually frightened, which again can lead to a dog fight. And there are even some people who intentionally bring aggressive dogs to a dog park to start a dog fight.

There is also the issue of owners so busy socializing with other owners that they don't pay attention to their dogs, which can be found actively guarding the park entrance and fence fighting with every new dog that enters the park.

There is rarely supervision to make sure all the dogs in the park are properly licensed and vaccinated, so disease can run rampant.

If there is a dog park near your home with a good reputation, or one where a friend attends regularly without incident, go and check it out a few times at different times of the day—without your Goldendoodle.

Never, ever take a puppy to a dog park. Generally, wait until your dog is at least twelve months old before heading to your local dog park, and then you should go only with a great deal of research and caution. Not all puppies and dogs are prepared for such an overwhelming experience. Not only can this be potentially dangerous, scary, and counterproductive to your training, but your puppy can be stepped on, bit, or rolled, leaving her with negative, long-term effects. If your Goldendoodle shakes, shivers, or hides, this is your cue she is not ready for this type of environment.

If you have a miniature Goldendoodle, check to see if there is a play area for small dogs near your home. This gives smaller dogs an opportunity to play with dogs their own size. Never have your small dog mixing and playing with bigger dogs—she can be seriously injured.

Doggy Daycares

Doggy daycare can be a great place to socialize your Goldendoodle. However, eight hours a day is too long for a new puppy to spend at daycare, so start with a half day, two or three times a week. Not all daycare facilities are created equal, so before enrolling your puppy, get recommendations from your veterinarian. Then visit a few facilities and ask questions.

Dog Walkers

Hiring a dog walker to take your puppy for walks is another great way to socialize and train your dog. This keeps her on track with housetraining while you are away for long periods during the day. Today's video technology allows you to see when the dog walker arrives and how he/she interacts with your dog. A GPS tracker on your Goldendoodle's collar lets you track where, and for how long, your dog is being walked.

Activities

With her many intrinsic talents,
your Goldendoodle has a world
of opportunities open to her!

There are any number of things you and your Goldendoodle can do together. Your Goldendoodle's intelligence and athleticism make her perfect for just about any type of work or activity. And size does not matter; any size Goldendoodle can participate. Your Mini Goldendoodle may be the next dock diving champion!

AKC CANINE PARTNERS

The AKC Canine Partners program allows your Goldendoodle to participate in a variety of AKC sports and certifications, from the quiet, gentle world of therapy work to the wild sport of dock diving—and a long list of activities in between.

AKC CANINE GOOD CITIZEN (CGC)

This certification program is a ten-step test designed to test your Goldendoodle's manners at home and in the community at large. Passing the CGC is required if you want to pursue other canine endeavors with your Goldendoodle, such as therapy work or search and rescue.

AKC THERAPY CERTIFICATION TRAINING

If your Goldendoodle has the right temperament, providing therapy dog services to nursing homes, children's homes, hospitals, hospices, libraries, and other settings is rewarding work. Therapy dog certification varies from state to state.

SEARCH AND RESCUE

Search and Rescue work, both urban and wilderness, requires an intelligent dog and a dedicated handler. The training is intense and long, and the work is difficult, but it can be extremely rewarding. Search and rescue dogs are not just used for the big disasters seen on television, but also for the small, personal disasters, such as locating a missing child or an Alzheimer's patient who has wandered from home. Your local police or fire department can put you in touch with a local training facility, or you can train through the AKC programs.

RALLY OBEDIENCE

Rally Obedience is loads of fun and a good entry point into dog sports. Your Goldendoodle can excel in competitive obedience. Even before she passes her CGC, she can participate in local competitive obedience trials, where her obedience skills and your training are judged. As she progresses, she can compete in more difficult trials.

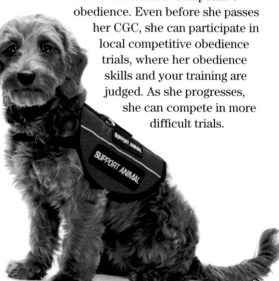

AGILITY

Agility competition is a race through an obstacle course. Your Goldendoodle is off leash and directed through the obstacle course by you, without the aid of food or toy enticements. Agility is physically and intellectually challenging for both you and your Goldendoodle, requiring a high level of teamwork and communication. It is not recommended until a dog is twelve months old and has sound hips, elbows, and patellas.

TRICKS

Teaching your Goldendoodle to do tricks is easy and a lot of fun. You can either learn them from a book or Internet videos, or you can take a tricks class. It is a great way to keep your Goldendoodle mentally challenged and your friends and family entertained. You can also compete in four levels of AKC Tricks competitions.

OUTDOOR ADVENTURES

Your Goldendoodle is an athletic dog bred from sporting dogs who spent their days in the field retrieving game. She'll happily accompany you on your outdoor adventures. As with people, it is never a good idea to take a couch potato on a five-mile hike. Be sure your Goldendoodle is in good physical shape to participate and equip her with the appropriate gear for the environment.

DOCK DIVING

Your dog waits on a 40-foot (12-m) dock. You fling her favorite toy, and then, on your command, she hurtles down the dock, leaps off the end, and then lands in the water to retrieve her precious toy. Could anything be more fun for you and your dog? The dog who leaps the farthest is the winner, but the fun the two of you will have makes everyone a winner.

In 2014, the AKC began recognizing titles from the sanctioned dock diving governing body, North America Diving Dogs (NADD).

Caring for Your Aging Goldendoodle

Being prepared for your Goldendoodle's
senior years will help her age gracefully
and bring many treasured moments.

There is a long history between you and your elderly dog; she has been reading your body language for years and seldom needs instructions to know what you want or what is going to happen next. It is an easy, comfortable relationship.

When your Goldendoodle reaches eight or nine years old, she is classified as a geriatric dog. Because your Goldendoodle's health can change quickly as she ages, your veterinarian will change her check-up schedule from once a year to twice a year.

GOOD NUTRITION

Good nutrition is important throughout your Goldendoodle's life; however, it becomes even more critical as she ages. A senior dog cannot metabolize and/or digest foods as well as a young dog. Nutrients need to be of the highest grade.

Your Goldendoodle's digestive system may become more sensitive as she ages, so make any dietary changes carefully and with the help of your veterinarian. Limit food and treats to only high-quality products that have a limited number of artificial ingredients.

Your veterinarian may suggest supplements and other alternative treatments to help your Goldendoodle maintain her youthfulness as long as possible.

KEEP HER LEAN

As she ages, your Goldendoodle is naturally going to slow down. This decline in activity needs a corresponding decline in caloric intake. Extra weight has a serious impact on a senior dog's health and mobility. Not only does extra weight place added strain

Baseline Blood Work

It is critical to have comprehensive, baseline blood work done when your Goldendoodle reaches the age of seven— no later than age eight. This is the benchmark used to measure and determine geriatric changes in your dog.

on her joints, but it also places an extra burden on her aging heart.

EXERCISE–THE BODY

Motion is lotion for your aging dog's joints; however, exercising an elderly dog can be a challenge. She may start her walk at her usual pace, then slow down as the walk progresses. You need to be aware of how far she can go before she gets too tired. It is no fun, for you or your dog, to carry home (if you even can) an overtired, old dog, or to try to coax along an old girl who just wants to lie down in the grass and take a nap. Although it is important for your aging Goldendoodle to get daily exercise, it is equally important to not overdo it.

If you have access to a pool or calm water, swimming is excellent exercise for old joints. Just be sure she wears a floatation vest with a handle on top so you can grab her if needed.

Although she may not be up for chasing balls anymore, it doesn't mean she won't enjoy a few gentle tosses, a meander to pick up the ball, and then, when she's had enough, a nice rest in her favorite spot with her ball proudly held between her front paws.

EXERCISE—THE MIND

Keeping your aging Goldendoodle mentally stimulated is just as important as keeping her joints moving. To keep her sharp, go through her commands on a soft, carpeted area. Give her puzzle toys on one of her nice orthopedic beds. Hide a treat in your hand, then hold out both fists to her and reward her when she touches the hand with the treat.

BEHAVIORAL CHANGES

As she ages, you will notice small, gradual changes in your Goldendoodle. She will become less active, more sedentary, and sleep longer and more soundly. She may appear to be confused when awakened and irritable if disturbed. She may lose interest in all but her favorite activities.

Your aging Goldendoodle is going to be less adaptable to change; make alterations in her daily routine slowly. Visitors, particularly children, need to approach her slowly, handle her gently, and understand if she decides to walk away from them. Your elderly Goldendoodle finds great comfort in being in the company of her family. Make sure her beds are near the hub of the family's activities.

When you travel, your old girl may be less tolerant of going to the boarding kennel. If possible, have a friend come and stay at the house with her instead. Staying in her home is a lot less stressful for her.

Your veterinarian is an important partner as you both work to navigate your Goldendoodle's senior years. If you notice any of the following behavioral changes, discuss them with your veterinarian to determine if they originate with a physical ailment or are signs of possible cognitive degeneration.

- Increased reaction to sounds
- Increased vocalization
- Confusion
- Disorientation
- Decreased interaction with humans
- Increased irritability
- Decreased response to commands
- Increased aggressive/protective behavior
- Increased anxiety
- House soiling
- Decreased self-hygiene/grooming
- Repetitive activity
- Increased wandering
- Change in sleep cycles

PHYSICAL CHANGES

Arthritis develops as your dog ages, particularly if she is a larger Goldendoodle. Weight control and regular, moderate exercise go a long way toward keeping her joints moving with minimal pain. However, there may come a point where she needs some relief. Work with your veterinarian, beginning with nutraceutical joint supplements. Be aware that when you begin giving your dog medications, particularly pain relievers, they can have side effects, including liver damage. Arthritis pain can make your dog irritable, so it is important to do what you can to ease her discomfort.

Your Goldendoodle will have a lower tolerance for extremes of hot and cold, so place beds in areas of the room/house where the temperature is moderate, consistent, and away from any drafts.

As your Goldendoodle ages, her hearing diminishes. This often makes it necessary to change from verbal commands to hand signals; if you continued hand signals from puppyhood, the decline in hearing becomes much less stressful on both of you.

Her visual acuity may also lessen over time, so if you notice her vision is failing, try not to move the furniture. She has a mental map of her home that allows her to move about without bumping into anything.

MAKE HER COMFORTABLE

Geriatric dogs often need special gear. Orthopedic beds provide support for aging, arthritic joints. Also, depending on where you live, consider a heated bed. Keeping her warm helps her mobility and quality of life.

At a minimum, invest in a ramp to help her move easily in and out of your car. This saves her joints from the impact of jumping and your back from the task of lifting her. If she is used to being on the furniture with you or sleeping on your bed, consider getting her a set of stairs to climb up and down. Although it may seem a very short distance from the couch to the floor, the impact on her front elbow joints can, over time, be debilitating.

You may also want to have her fitted for a vest or harness with a handle, so you can provide guidance and support without interfering with her forward motion.

MEDICATIONS

Elderly dogs will often have one or two prescriptions, along with joint supplements.

It is important for everyone in the family to be clear about how and when her medications and supplements are to be administered. Write this all out and keep the list of

instructions with the medications. (Keep all canine medications and supplements out of reach of children.) You never know when an emergency may require a friend to feed and medicate your elderly Goldendoodle. Written instructions make it easier for you, your friend, and your dog.

A Word of Caution

Make your veterinarian aware of ALL medications and supplements your Goldendoodle is taking. Without the training and experience of your veterinarian, you may create a nutritional perfect storm in your dog's body, potentially putting her health at great risk.

Information

USEFUL ADDRESSES AND CONTACTS

Veterinary Organizations

American Veterinary Medical Association
www.avma.org

The American Holistic Veterinary Medical
Association
www.ahvma.org

American College of Veterinary
Ophthalmologists
www.acvo.com

Orthopedic Foundation for Animals (OFA)
www.ofa.org

PennHIP
www.pennhip.org

ASPCA
American Society for the Prevention of
Cruelty to Animals (ASPCA)
www.aspca.org

ASPCA Animal Poison Control Center
(888) 426-4435
(There is a consultation fee for this service.)

ASPCA Poison App
Search your app store for Animal Poison by
ASPCA.

Canine Health Studies

Cancer Research—GRCA
www.grca.org/about-the-breed/health-research
Early Spay and Neuter
www.grca.org/wp-content/uploads/2015/08/EffectsEarlySpayNeuterPurina1.pdf

Early Spay Neuter Study
www.grca.org/about-the-breed/health-research/effects-of-early-spay-or-neuter-in-golden-retrievers

Goldendoodle Organizations

Goldendoodle Association of North America
(GANA)
www.goldendoodleassociation.com

Goldendoodle and Labradoodle Breeders List
www.goldendoodle-labradoodle.org

The Goldendoodle Website and Forum
www.goldendoodles.com

Goldendoodle Rescue and Rehome Organizations

IDOG Rescue /Rehome Resources
Rescuing and Rehoming Labradoodles and
Goldendoodles throughout North America
www.idogrescue.com

The Doodle Rescue Collective
www.doodlerescuecollective.com

Discussion Forums
The Doodle Zoo
www.thedoodlezoo.com

The Goldendoodle Website and Forum
www.goldendoodles.com

Facebook: Goldendoodle Dog Owners Group
www.facebook.com/groups/2245481911

Grooming Instructions
IDOG Rescue Grooming Guide
www.idogrescue.com/grooming_guide

Dog Trainer Certification Organizations
Association of Professional Dog Trainers
www.apdt.com

Certification Council for Professional
Dog Trainers
www.ccpdt.org

Activities
AKC Canine Partners
*www.akc.org/register/information/
canine-partners*

Dock Diving
North America Diving Dogs (NADD)
www.northamericadivingdogs.com

Agility
North American Dog Agility Council
(NADAC)
www.nadac.com

United States Dog Agility Association
(USDAA)
www.usdaa.com

Tricks
AKC Tricks Competition
www.akc.org/sports/trick-dog

Articles
Puppy/cat introductions
*https://www.petmd.com/blogs/thedailyvet/
lhuston/2012/mar/introduce_new_puppy_
to_cat-13443*

Books
Eldredge, Debra, *et al. Dog Owner's Home Veterinary Handbook.* Hoboken, NJ: Wiley Publishing, Inc., 2007
Fennell, Jan. *The Dog Listener.* New York, NY: HarperCollins Publishers, Inc., 2004
McConnell, Patricia, Ph.D. *The Other End of the Leash.* New York, NY: Random House Publishing Group, 2002
Yin, Sophia. *How to Behave So Your Dog Behaves.* Neptune, NJ: T. F. H. Publications, Inc., 2004

Important Note

This pet owner's manual tells the reader how to buy or adopt, and care for, a Goldendoodle. The author and publisher consider it important to point out that the advice given in the book is meant primarily for normally developed dogs of excellent physical health and sound temperament.

Anyone who acquires a fully grown dog should be aware that the animal has already formed its basic impressions of human beings. The new owner should watch the animal carefully, including its behavior toward humans, and, whenever possible, should meet the previous owner.

Caution is further advised in the association of children with dogs, in meeting with other dogs, and in exercising the dog without a leash.

Even well-behaved and carefully supervised dogs sometimes do damage to someone else's property or cause accidents. It is therefore in the owner's interest to be adequately insured against such eventualities, and we strongly urge all dog owners to purchase a liability policy that covers their dog.

Index

Dedicated to Carol Vizcarra and her two Goldendoodle boys in heaven, Archie and Bruno.

About the Author

Edie MacKenzie has owned hybrid dogs exclusively since 1985 and is one of the leading authors on the special care needed when purchasing a hybrid or designer dog. With particular consideration given to "never owned a dog before" dog owners, she walks her readers through the ins and outs of life with dogs. Her books include *Barron's Goldendoodles: A Complete Pet Owner's Manual, Barron's Dog Bible: Golden Retrievers, The Definitive Guide to Labradoodles, The Definitive Guide to Goldendoodles, The Definitive Guide to Puggles, Your Doodle Puppy's First Year Made Easy,* and *The Perfect Little Training Guide for the Imperfect Owner.* Her books have sold on every continent but Antarctica. She has written numerous articles and blog posts, many of which can be found on her website, *www.ediemackenzie.com.* Edie lives in Texas with her husband; two Australian Labradoodles, Wally and Murphy; eight tortoises; and an Eastern box turtle named Ebby.

A Note on Pronouns

Many dog lovers feel that the pronoun "it" is not appropriate when referring to a beloved pet. For this reason, Goldendoodles are referred to as "she" throughout this book, unless the topic specifically relates to male dogs. No gender bias is intended by this writing style.

Photo Credits

Tara Darling: page 93

iStock: cpaquin: page 82; Laura Fay: page 2; Hannahmariah: pages 8, 90; Jbssfelix: pages 32; jimmyjamesbond: page 50; Michael Krinke: pages 47, 83; nycshooter: pages 13, 18, 23, 40, 80 (top); Steve Debenport: page 44

Andrea Johnson: page 86

Shutterstock: anetapics: pages 20, 28; Ashley Marie Violette: page 80 (bottom); Daniel Brachlow: page 67; Deanna Oliva Kelly: page 56; Dennis Wegewijs: page 64; everydoghasastory: pages 25, 35; haeryung stock images: pages 37, 39, 49, 85; Hannahmariah: page 31; iofoto: page 24; Jaden Sorenson: page 14; Sylvie Bouchard: page 33; Tamara Ray: page 38; Thomas Nord: page 81; Tom Biegalski: page 7; Tracey Patterson: page 57

Carol Vizcarra: pages 4, 11, 16, 17, 59, 63, 65, 89

Connie Summers/Paulette Johnson: page 6

Woof Tracks Photography: pages 10, 26, 34, 36, 42, 68, 70, 71, 74, 77

Cover Photos

Front cover: Carol Vizcarra (left), Carol Vizcarra (top right), Shutterstock: anetapics (center right), Carol Vizcarra (bottom right)

Back cover: Shutterstock: anetapics

Inside front cover: Shutterstock: anetapics

Inside back cover: Andrea Johnson

All inquiries should be addressed to:
B.E.S. Publishing Co.
250 Wireless Boulevard
Hauppauge, NY 11788
www.bes-publishing.com

ISBN: 978-1-4380-1162-2

Library of Congress Control No.: 2018947051

Printed in China
9 8 7 6 5 4 3 2 1